D0504090

The Observers Series
AIRCRAFT

About the Book

Observers Aircraft is the indispensable pocket guide to the world's latest aeroplanes, helicopters and tilt-rotor aircraft, and the most recent versions of established types. This, the thirty-ninth edition, embraces the latest civil and military aeroplanes and rotorcraft of twenty countries. Its scope ranges from such airliner newcomers as the Airbus A340, the BAe Jetstream 41, the Canadair RJ and the Deutsche Aerospace (Do) 328, through general aviation débutantes, such as the BAe 1000, the Pilatus PC-12 and the Swearingen-Jaffe SJ 30, to a variety of new military aircraft that include the McDonnell Douglas C-17A heavy lift freighter, the Chinese NAMC K-8 basic trainer and light attack aircraft, and the configurationally innovative YF-22 and YF-23, competing, as this edition closed for press, to fulfil the USAF's Advanced Tactical Fighter requirement. All data has been checked and revised as necessary, and more than seventy-five per cent of the three-view silhouettes are new or have been revised for this edition.

About the Author

William Green, compiler of *Observers Aircraft* for forty years, is internationally known for many works of aviation reference. He entered aviation journalism during the early years of World War II, subsequently serving with the Royal Air Force and resuming aviation writing in 1947. Until recently, William Green was managing editor of the monthly *AIR International*, one of the largest-circulation European-based aviation journals, and co-editor of its thrice-annual companion publication, *AIR Enthusiast*.

The *Observer's* series was launched in 1937 with the publication of *The Observer's Book of Birds*. Today, over fifty years later, paperback *Observers* continue to offer practical, useful information on a wide range of subjects, and with every book regularly revised by experts, the facts are right up-to-date. Students, amateur enthusiasts and professional organisations alike will find the latest *Observers* invaluable.

'Thick and glossy, briskly informative' – *The Guardian*

'If you are a serious spotter of any of the things the series deals with, the books must be indispensable' – *The Times Educational Supplement*

◉ O B S E R V E R S

AIRCRAFT

William Green

With silhouettes by Dennis Punnett

BLOOMSBURY BOOKS
LONDON

PENGUIN BOOKS

Published by the Penguin Group
Penguin Books Ltd, 27 Wrights Lane, London W8 5TZ, England
Penguin Books USA Inc., 375 Hudson Street, New York, New York 10014, USA
Penguin Books Australia Ltd, Ringwood, Victoria, Australia
Penguin Books Canada Ltd, 10 Alcorn Avenue, Toronto, Ontario, Canada M4V 3B2
Penguin Books (NZ) Ltd, 182–190 Wairau Road, Auckland 10, New Zealand

Penguin Books Ltd, Registered Offices: Harmondsworth, Middlesex, England

Thirty-ninth edition 1991
Fourtieth edition 1992

This edition published by Bloomsbury Books, an imprint of
The Godfrey Cave Group, 42 Bloomsbury Street, London, WC1B 3QJ,
under licence from Penguin Books Limited, 1993

1 3 5 7 9 10 8 6 4 2

Copyright © Frederick Warne & Co. Ltd. 1991, 1992

Printed and bound in Great Britain by
BPCC Hazell Books Ltd
Member of BPCC Ltd

ISBN 1 85471 144 X

INTRODUCTION TO THE 1992/93 EDITION

WITH THIS EDITION, *Observers Aircraft* completes 40 years as an annual pocket reference. Four decades represent a long span of time in terms of aeronautical evolution, embracing, as they do, almost half the annals of manned wingborne powered flight. It is scarcely surprising, therefore, that not one aircraft appearing in the first annual *Observers Aircraft* is to be found in any shape or form in this, the fortieth edition. Indeed, fewer than a dozen of the types in that 1952 *Observers Aircraft* are still to be seen in the world's skies, these including such veterans as the DC-3 and T-6 Texan, the Canberra and the Hunter. In that original edition there appeared but one turbojet-driven airliner and merely two utilising turboprops, *piston*-engined aircraft preponderating.

Comparatively early in its existence, the proliferation of new military aircraft resulting from the pressures of the so-called 'cold war' and of new commercial aircraft to cater for the rapid worldwide expansion of airliner operations dictated a major change in *Observers Aircraft*. From a modest pocket guide to the world's *principal* aircraft it metamorphosised to a reference work to the *latest* types under test or in production. But further evolution may well prove necessary in the future; change perhaps foretokened by this edition which contains fewer entirely *new* aircraft than any of its predecessors. Consisting solely of the Eurofighter and the Yak-141, these newcomers are accompanied by a dozen or so other *new* types that are effectively *derivatives*.

Factors influencing and accelerating the decline in the rate of development of completely new aircraft include the recent demise of the Soviet Union and global recession. The former is having a devastating effect on the once-immense eastern *bloc* aviation industry, while, in the west, the decline in demand for defence products in which it has resulted in dramatically reducing both existing and projected military aircraft programmes. Furthermore, aviation research and development, traditionally supported by the defence sector, is being cut back. On the commercial side, few aircraft categories are proving immune to prevalent unfavourable market conditions, and, as this *Observers Aircraft* closes for press, rare is the manufacturer able to take comfort from its order books. Research and development in the civil sector is funded from manufacturing profits, which, at present, are regrettably proscribed. Ergo: fewer entirely new aircraft types, military or civil, in the years ahead!

WILLIAM GREEN

AERO L 59 (L 39MS)

Country of Origin: Czechoslovakia.
Type: Tandem two-seat basic and advanced trainer.
Power Plant: One 4,852 lb st (21·57 kN) ZMKB (Progress)/ ZVL DV-2 turbofan.
Performance: Max speed, 544 mph (876 km/h) at 16,405 ft (5 000 m); max initial climb, 5,120 ft/min (26 m/sec); service ceiling, 38,500 ft (11 730 m); range (max external fuel), 932 mls (1 500 km) at 29,530 ft (9 000 m).
Weights: Empty, 9,149 lb (4 150 kg); loaded, 12,566 lb (5 700 kg); max permissible takeoff, 15,432 lb (7 000 kg).
Armament: One 23-mm GSh-23 twin-barrel cannon in fuselage pod and four wing stations for such ordnance loads as four 220-lb (100-kg) and two 551-lb (250-kg) bombs.
Status: First pre-series L 59 flown 1 October 1989, this being preceded by five prototypes. The first announced customer for the L 59 is Egypt, which, in 1991, placed a contract for 48 as lead-in fighter trainers for 1992 delivery.
Notes: The L 59 (formerly known as the L 39MS) is a second generation derivative of the L 39 Albatros first flown in prototype form on 4 November 1968 and of which 2,130 had been built for the Soviet Union and some 700 more for indigenous use and for export to a dozen countries. The L 59 mates a new engine (replacing the AI-25TL) with revised wing, new avionics, a new undercarriage and zero-zero ejection seats. Production of the L 39 continues in parallel with the L 59 (Nigeria having ordered 30 and the Philippines 18 during 1991), and a further derivative, the L 139 was being offered at the beginning of 1992 with a 4,000 lb st (17·79 kN) Garrett TFE 731-4 turbofan and similar Western avionics to those being installed in the L 59 and recent export L 39s.

AERO L 59 (L 39MS)

Dimensions: Span (including tip tanks), 31 ft $3\frac{1}{2}$ in (9,54 m); length, 40 ft $0\frac{1}{4}$ in (12,20 m); height, 15 ft $8\frac{1}{4}$ in (4,78 m); wing area, 202·37 sq ft (18,80 m²).

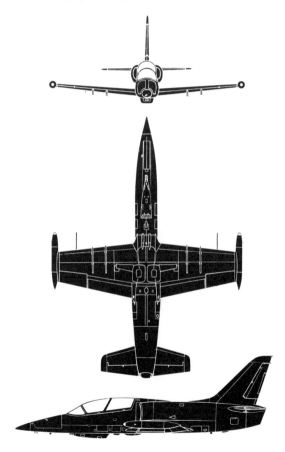

AGUSTA (SIAI MARCHETTI) S.211

Country of Origin: Italy.
Type: Tandem two-seat basic trainer.
Power Plant: One 2,500 lb st (11·13 kN) Pratt & Whitney Canada JT15D-4C turbofan.
Performance: Max speed, 414 mph (667 km/h) at 25,000 ft (7 620 m); range cruise, 311 mph (500 km/h) at 30,000 ft (9 150 m); max initial climb, 4,200 ft/min (21,34 m/sec); service ceiling, 40,000 ft (12 200 m); max range (internal fuel), 1,036 mls (1 668 km); ferry range (two 77 Imp gal/350 l external tanks), 1,543 mls (2 483 km).
Weights: Empty, 4,078 lb (1 850 kg); max take-off (training mission), 6,063 lb (2 750 kg), (max external ordnance), 6,944 lb (3 150 kg).
Armament: (Weapons training and light attack) Four wing stations each stressed for 727·5 lb (330 kg) inboard and 364 lb (165 kg) outboard. Max external ordnance load of 1,455 lb (660 kg). Typical loads may include two 20-mm or four 12,7-mm gun pods, four 18 × 50-mm, 7 × 2·75-in or 6 × 68-mm rockets, or four bombs each of up to 330 lb (150 kg).
Status: First of three prototypes flown 10 April 1981, and first production aircraft (for Singapore) flown on 4 October 1984. Six aircraft supplied complete and 24 as CKD kits to Singapore, and four complete aircraft and 14 as CKD kits delivered to the Philippines. Four supplied to Haiti, but subsequently resold in the USA, and four ordered by Brunei for mid-1992 delivery.
Notes: Agusta in partnership with Grumman is proposing an upgraded S.211 as a candidate for the JPATS (USAF and USN Joint Primary Aircraft Training System) contest. The S.211 is also being offered with an uprated JT15D engine, increased fuel, an Omega navigation computer and a head-up display.

AGUSTA (SIAI MARCHETTI) S.211

Dimensions: Span, 27 ft 8 in (8,43 m); length, 30 ft 6½ in (9,31 m); height, 12 ft 5½ in (3,80 m); wing area, 135·63 sq ft (12,60 m²).

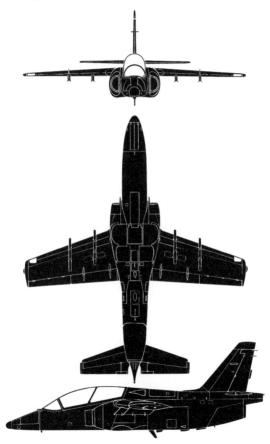

AIDC A-1 CHING-KUO

Country of Origin: Taiwan.

Type: Single-seat air defence fighter.

Power Plant: Two 5,000 lb st (22·24 kN) dry and 9,460 lb st (42·08 kN) afterburning ITEC (Garrett) TFE1042-70 turbofans.

Performance: No data have been released at the time of closing for press, but maximum speed is expected to range from 800 mph (1 285 km/h) at sea level, or Mach = 1·05, to 1,385 mph (2 230 km/h) above 36,000 ft (10 975 m), or Mach = 2·1.

Weights: No details available for publication.

Armament: One 20-mm M61A Vulcan rotary cannon and (intercept) four Sky Sword I short-range and two Sky Sword II medium-range AAMs. Max external ordnance load (distributed between two wingtip, four underwing and two fuselage centreline stores stations) is 9,000 lb (4 082 kg).

Status: First of four prototypes of the Ching-kuo (three single-seat and one two-seat) was flown on 28 May 1989, all remaining three having joined the flight test programme by the beginning of 1991. First series production aircraft (a two-seat B version) was delivered in April 1992 against initial contract for 60 aircraft placed in 1990. Contract for second batch of 60 was expected to be finalised by mid 1992 when procurement of 250 aircraft by the year 2000 was planned.

Notes: Named after a former president of Taiwan, Chiang Ching-kuo, the A-1 has been developed by AIDC (Aero Industry Development Centre) with General Dynamics under the Ying Yang (Soaring Eagle) programme. The Garrett engines are manufactured in Taiwan by ITEC (International Turbo Engine Company) under the Yan Han (Cloud Man) programme. It is anticipated that third and subsequent production orders for the A-1 will involve an upgraded version powered by ITEC F125X engines with ratings of 12,500 lb st (56 kN).

AIDC A-1 CHING-KUO

Dimensions: No details available for publication.

AIRBUS A300-600R

Country of Origin: International consortium.
Type: Medium- to long-haul commercial transport.
Power Plant: Two 59,000 lb st (262·4 kN) General Electric CF6-80C2A1 or 61,500 lb st (273·6 kN) CF6-80C2A5 turbofans, or 56,000 lb st (249 kN) Pratt & Whitney PW4156 or 58,000 lb st (258 kN) PW4158 turbofans.
Performance: Max cruise, 557 mph (897 km/h) at 30,000 ft (9 150 m); long-range cruise, 543 mph (875 km/h) at 31,000 ft (9 450 m); range (standard fuel and CF6 engines), 4,664 mls (7 505 km), (PW4156/8 engines), 4,870 mls (7 840 km).
Weights: Operational empty (CF6), 197,686 lb (89 670 kg), (PW4156/8), 197,523 lb (89 595 kg); max take-off, 375,885 lb (170 500 kg) or (option) 378,535 lb (171 700 kg).
Accommodation: Typical mixed-class arrangement for 26 first-class, six abreast, and 241 economy-class, eight abreast.
Status: First A300 flown on 28 October 1972, and first -600 version flown on 8 July 1983, with extended-range -600R following on 9 December 1987. Deliveries of the -600R commenced (to American Airlines) on 21 April 1988. Total of 457 A300s (all versions) ordered by beginning of 1992, with 364 delivered. Sales of variants prior to -600/-600R totalled 248.
Notes: The A300, like all the subsequent Airbus types, is manufactured by a consortium of Aérospatiale (France), Deutsche Aerospace (Germany), British Aerospace (UK), Fokker (Netherlands) and CASA (Spain). Current A300 production consists of the -600 and -600R versions, and deliveries of a -600F dedicated freighting version will begin in 1994, to Federal Express.

12

AIRBUS A300-600R

Dimensions: Span, 147 ft 1¼ in (44,84 m); length, 177 ft 5 in (54,08 m); height, 54 ft 6½ in (16,62 m); wing area, 2,798·7 sq ft (260,00 m²).

AIRBUS A310-300

Country of Origin: International consortium.

Type: Short- to medium-haul commercial transport.

Power Plant: Two 53,500 lb st (238 kN) General Electric CF6-80C2A2 or 59,000 lb st (262·4 kN) CF6-80C2A8 turbofans, or 52,000 lb st (231·2 kN) Pratt & Whitney PW4152 or 56,000 lb st (249·1 kN) PW4156A turbofans.

Performance: Max cruise speed, 557 mph (897 km/h) at 35,000 ft (10 670 m); long-range cruise, 528 mph (850 km/h) at 37,000 ft (11 280 m); range with 218 passengers and international reserves (CF6-80C2A2 engines), 5,090 mls (8 191 km), (PW4152 engines), 5,160 mls (8 300 km).

Weights: Typical operational empty, 177,000 lb (80 300 kg); max take-off, 330,695 lb (150 000 kg) or (option) 361,560 lb (164 000 kg).

Accommodation: Flight crew of two (with provision for third and fourth crew seats) and maximum capacity for up to 280 passengers nine abreast. Typical two-class layout for 20 first-class passengers six abreast and 192 economy-class passengers eight abreast.

Status: Prototype flown 3 April 1982, and first deliveries (Lufthansa and Swissair) commencing 29 March 1983. Extended range -300 version first flown 8 July 1985, with deliveries commencing (to Swissair) on following 17 December. Total of 251 A310s (all versions) sold by early 1992 and 205 delivered, including 85 of the -200, which is no longer in production.

Notes: By comparison with the A300, the A310 has a new wing of reduced size and a shorter fuselage. The -300 version introduced an additional fuel tank in the tailplane. A310C convertible and A310F all-freight versions are also in service.

AIRBUS A310-300

Dimensions: Span, 144 ft 0 in (43,90 m); length, 153 ft 1 in (46,66 m); height, 51 ft 10 in (15,81 m); wing area, 2,357·3 sq ft (219,00 m²).

AIRBUS A321

Country of Origin: International consortium.
Type: Short- to medium-haul commercial transport.
Power Plant: Two 30,000 lb st (133·4 kN) CFM56-5B1 or IAE V2530-A5 or 31,000 lb st (138 kN) CFM56-5B2 turbofans.
Performance: Max cruise speed, 560 mph (903 km/h) at 28,000 ft (8 535 m); econ cruise, 514 mph (828 km/h) at 37,000 ft (11 280 m); range (186 passengers and typical reserves), 2,700 mls (4 350 km).
Weights: Operational empty, 103,400 lb (46 900 kg); max take-off, 181,200 lb (82 200 kg).
Accommodation: Flight crew of two and maximum seating for 220 passengers six abreast, depending on layout. Typical two-class arrangement provides for 16 first-class and 170 economy-class passengers, respectively four and six abreast.
Status: A321 was launched on 24 November 1989 as a stretched version of the A320, trading range for extra passenger capacity. First (of four) flight-test aircraft to enter flight development in March 1993, with two each to fly with CFM56-5B1 and V2530-A5 engines. Certification and entry into service at the beginning of 1994. Firm orders for 140 placed by 10 airlines by the beginning of 1992.
Notes: The A321 is the first 'stretch' of the A320, itself the smallest of the Airbus range when it entered service in 1988. Fuselage 'plugs' ahead of and behind the wing increase the fuselage length by 14 ft (4,27 m), allowing, typically, 36 more passengers to be accommodated in six rows. The A321 is being developed on the basis of 'minimum change' from the A320-200, principal differences apart from the extra length being a strengthened undercarriage for the higher weights, more powerful engines and a modified wing with double slotted flaps.

AIRBUS A330

Dimensions: Span, 197 ft 10 in (60,30 m); length, 208 ft 11¾ in (63,70 m); height, 55 ft 2 in (16,83 m); wing area, 3,908·4 sq ft (363,10 m²).

AIRBUS A340

Country of Origin: International consortium.
Type: Long-haul commercial transport.
Power Plant: Four 31,200 lb st (138·8 kN) CFM International CFM56-5C2 or 32,550 lb st (145 kN) CFM56-5C3 turbofans.
Performance: (Estimated, -300) Max cruise speed, 575 mph (914 km/h) at 33,000 ft (10 060 m); econ cruise, 547 mph (880 km/h) at 39,000 ft (11 890 m); max operating altitude, 41,000 ft (12 500 m); range (with 295 passengers), 7,700 mls (12 500 km); range, (high gross weight option), 8,200 mls (126 300 km).
Weights: (-300) Operational empty, 278,450 lb (126 300 kg); max take-off, 558,900 lb (253 500 kg); optional high-gross weight, 588,620 lb (267 000 kg).
Accommodation: Flight crew of two and (-300) typical three-class arrangement for 18 first, 81 business and 196 economy class passengers in six-, seven- and eight-abreast seating, all with twin aisles. Maximum of 440 passengers nine abreast.
Status: Launched on 5 June 1987 (in parallel with the A330), the A340 is offered in -200 and -300 versions, the latter being the first to fly, on 25 October 1991, joined by second on 3 February 1992. First -200 (third of the six-aircraft test fleet) to fly late-March 1992. Certification and first deliveries (both models) in first quarter 1993. Total firm orders for 115 by early 1992.
Notes: The A340 is being developed in parallel with the twin-engined A330 (see previous page) which has wing, cockpit and tail commonality, and the same basic fuselage. The A340-200 is a very-long-range version, the A340-300 having its fuselage lengthened by 14 ft $1\frac{1}{4}$ in (4,30 m) and reduced range. The A340-300 Combi will typically carry six freight pallets and 194 passengers in a three-class layout. The A340-200X and A340-300X have uprated engines and higher operating weights, as noted above. Projected A340-400X will have a further fuselage stretch for 40 more passengers.

Dimensions: Span, 197 ft 10 in (60,30 m); length, 208 ft 11¾ in (63,70 m); height, 55 ft 2 in (16,83 m); wing area, 3,908·4 sq ft (363,10 m²).

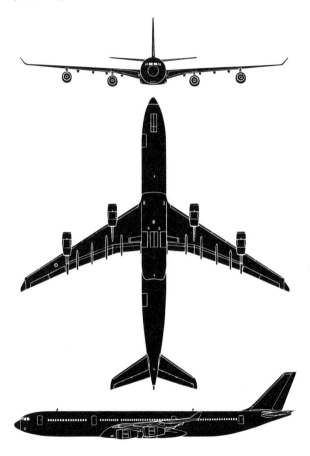

AIRTECH (CASA/IPTN) CN-235-100

Countries of Origin: Spain and Indonesia.
Type: Regional commercial transport, military freighter (CN-235 M) and maritime patrol aircraft (CN-235 MPA).
Power Plant: Two 1 750 hp (1,305 kW) General Electric CT7-9C turboprops.
Performance: (CN-235-100) Max cruise speed, 286 mph (460 km/h) at 15,000 ft (4 575 m); max initial climb, 1,527 ft/min (7,75 m/sec); service ceiling, 26,600 ft (8 110 m); range (with reserves at 18,000 ft/5 485 m), 518 mls (834 km) with max payload, 2,429 mls (3 910 km) with max fuel.
Weights: Operational empty, 21,605 lb (9 800 kg); max take-off, 33,290 lb (15 100 kg).
Accommodation: (Commercial version) Flight crew of two with basic arrangement for 45 passengers in four-abreast seating with central aisle. (CN-235 M) Forty-eight troops or 46 paratroops, or 24 casualty stretchers and four attendants. Quick Change version offers various combinations of passengers and standard LD2 or LD3 freight containers.
Status: First prototype flown (in Spain) on 11 November 1983 and second (in Indonesia) on 31 December 1983. First customer delivery (Merpati Nusantara) 15 December 1986. Orders at beginning of 1992 totalled 178 aircraft, including 50 to be asembled in Turkey. Of these, military orders totalled 137 aircraft (Botswana, Chile, Ecuador, France, Gabon, Indonesia, Ireland, Morocco, Panama, Saudi Arabia, Spain and Turkey). Production tempo of 20 aircraft annually.
Notes: The CN-235 is manufactured jointly by CASA in Spain and IPTN in Indonesia on a 50-50 basis without component duplication and through the jointly-owned Airtech. The CN-235 MPA maritime patrol version with forward-looking infrared and 360°-scan search radar entered flight test in 1991 and is illustrated opposite. Two have been ordered by Ireland.

AIRTECH (CASA/IPTN) CN-235-100

Dimensions: (CN-235-100) Span, 84 ft 7¾ in (25,81 m); length, 70 ft 0½ in (21,35 m); height, 26 ft 10 in (8,18 m); wing area, 636·17 sq ft (59,10 m²).

ALENIA C-27A (G222)

Country of Origin: Italy (USA).
Type: General-purpose military STOL transport.
Power Plant: Two 3,400 shp (2 535 kW) Fiat-built General Electric T64-GE-P4D turboprops.
Performance: (At 61,730 lb/28 000 kg) Max speed, 336 mph (540 km/h) at 15,000 ft (4 575 m); range cruise, 273 mph (439 km/h) at 19,680 ft (6 000 m); max initial climb, 1,705 ft/min (8,66 m/sec); time to 14,760 ft (4 500 m), 8·6 min; service ceiling, 25,000 ft (7 620 m); range (max payload), 852 mls (1 371 km); ferry range, 2,879 mls (4 633 km).
Weights: Empty, 32,165 lb (14 590 kg); max take-off, 61,730 lb (28 000 kg).
Accommodation: Normal crew of four (two pilots, radio operator/flight engineer and loadmaster) and up to 19,840 lb (9 000 kg) of freight. Five pallets of up to 2,205 lb (1 000 kg) each can be airdropped. As troop transport up to 53 fully-equipped troops may be carried.
Status: First of 10 G222s delivered to Chrysler Technologies Airborne Systems in the USA for conversion as C-27A in June 1991, with first delivery to USAF on following 16 August and second on 26 September. Deliveries continuing through 1992 with option on further 10 aircraft.
Notes: The G222 was selected as winning contender in a USAF competition for a medium-range pressurised airlift aircraft for service in Panama and Latin America. Chrysler Technologies Airborne Systems (CTAS) is US prime contractor for the aircraft which has been assigned the designation C-27A. CTAS is responsible for installing upgraded navigation, communication and mission systems, and the C-27As are to be used to transport military units and equipment to remote, unimproved airfields, utilising the aircraft's STOL capability.

ALENIA C-27A (G222)

Dimensions: Span, 94 ft 2 in (28,70 m); length, 74 ft 5½ in (22,70 m); height, 32 ft 1¾ in (9,80 m); wing area, 882·64 sq ft (82,00 m²).

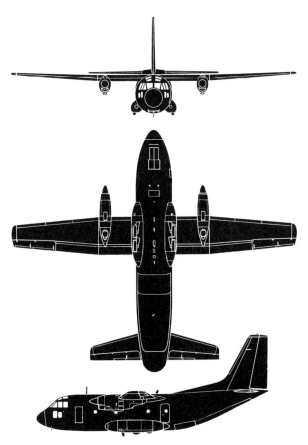

AMX INTERNATIONAL AMX

Countries of Origin: Italy and Brazil.

Type: Single-seat battlefield support aircraft.

Power Plant: One 11,030 lb st (49·1 kN) Rolls-Royce Spey Mk 807 turbofan.

Performance: Max speed (at 23,700 lb/10 750 kg), 568 mph (913 km/h) at 36,000 ft (10 975 m), or Mach = 0·86; max initial climb, 10,250 ft/min (52 m/sec); tactical radius (at 28,660 lb/13 000 kg), 328 mls (528 km) LO-LO-LO with 5 min combat and 10 per cent reserves, HI-LO-HI, 576 mls (926 km); ferry range (max external fuel and 10 per cent reserves), 2,073 mls (3 336 km).

Weights: Operational empty, 14,638 lb (6 640 kg); max take-off, 28,660 lb (13 000 kg).

Armament: One 20-mm rotary cannon (Italian) or two 30-mm cannon (Brazilian), two AIM-9L Sidewinder or similar self-defence AAMs. Max external ordnance load of 8,377 lb (3 800 kg).

Status: First of seven AMX prototypes flown (in Italy) 15 May 1984, two of these being assembled in Brazil with first flying on 16 October 1986. The first Italian series aircraft flown on 11 May 1988, and first Brazilian on 12 August 1989. First Italian AMX-T two-seater flown 14 March 1990 and first Brazilian on 14 August 1991. Planning at beginning of 1992 called for 187 single-seaters and 51 two-seaters for the Italian Air Force, and 65 single-seaters and 14 two-seaters for the Brazilian Air Force. Some 80 single- and two-seaters delivered to Italian Air Force by beginning of 1992, and approximately a dozen single-seaters to the Brazilian Air Force.

Notes: The AMX is being built by Alenia (46·7%) and Aermacchi (23·6%) in Italy and Embraer (29·7%) in Brazil, with three assembly lines and no component manufacturing duplication.

Dimensions: Span (over missiles), 32 ft $8\frac{1}{2}$ in (9,97 m); length, 43 ft $5\frac{1}{8}$ in (13,23 m); height, 14 ft $11\frac{1}{8}$ in (4,55 m); wing area, 226·04 sq ft (21,00 m²).

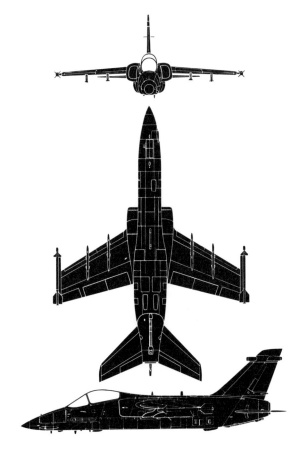

ANTONOV AN-74 (COALER)

Country of Origin: Commonwealth of Independent States (Ukraine).

Type: Light civil and military STOL transport.

Power Plant: Two 14,330 lb st (63·74 kN) ZMKB (Lotarev) D-36 or 16,545 lb st (73·6 kN) D-436K turbofans.

Performance: (D-36 turbofans) Max speed, 438 mph (705 km/h); normal cruise, 342 mph (550 km/h) at 32,800 ft (10 000 m); service ceiling, 32,810 ft (10 000 m); range (with 22,045-lb/10 000-kg payload and 2-hr reserve), 715 mls (1 150 km), (with 3,307-lb/1 500-kg payload), 2,610 mls (4 200 km).

Weights: Max take-off (from 3,280-ft/1 000-m runway), 60,625 lb (27 500 kg), or (from 5,905-ft/1 800-m runway), 76,060 lb (34 500 kg).

Accommodation: Pilot, co-pilot, navigator, radio operator and flight engineer on flight deck. Primarily for cargo loads, but cabin can be equipped with sidewall folding seats and removable central seats for 68 passengers, or 57 paratroops, or (medevac) 24 stretchers plus 12 seated casualties.

Status: First of two An-72 prototypes (Coaler-A) flown on 22 December 1977, with extensively revised pre-series (eight) An-72 (Coaler-C) following in 1985. This pre-series included two prototypes of the An-74 (Coaler-B). Series production at the rate of 20 annually (all versions) during 1991.

Notes: The An-72 and An-74 makes use of the 'Coanda effect' to achieve STOL performance, engine exhaust gases flowing over the wing upper surfaces and inboard slotted flaps. This configuration also reduces the risk of debris ingestion by the engines when operating from unprepared surfaces, for which both the An-72 and Arctic-dedicated An-74 were designed.

Dimensions: Span, 104 ft 7½ in (31,89 m); length, 92 ft 1¼ in (28,07 m); height, 28 ft 4½ in (8,65 m); wing area, 1,061·57 sq ft (98,62 m²).

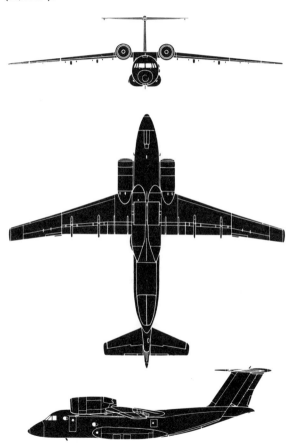

ATR (AEROSPATIALE/ALENIA) ATR 42

Countries of Origin: France and Italy.
Type: Short-range regional transport.
Power plant: Two flat-rated 1,800 shp (1 342 kW) Pratt & Whitney Canada PW120 or 1,950 shp (1 454 kW) PW121 turboprops.
Performance (ATR 42-300): Max cruise speed, 305 mph (490 km/h) at 17,000 ft (5 180 m); range with max payload, 1,210 mls (1 946 km); range with max fuel, 2,785 mls (4 481 km).
Weights: Operational empty, 22,674 lb (10 285 kg); max take-off, 36,817 lb (16 700 kg).
Accommodation: Flight crew of two and up to 50 passengers four abreast with single aisle at 30-in (76-cm) pitch.
Status: Two prototype/development aircraft, first flown 16 August and 31 October 1984. First production ATR 42 flown 30 April 1985. French certification of ATR 42-200 and ATR 42-300 on 25 September 1985, and first services flown by Air Littoral on 9 December. Stretched-fuselage ATR 72 flown on 27 October 1988; certification 25 September and first delivery (to Kar Air) 27 October 1989. Total sales by early 1992, 271 ATR 42 and 127 ATR 72; deliveries 221 and 51 respectively.
Notes: Collaborative programme for this Avion de Transport Regional (hence ATR) between Aérospatiale (France) and Aeritalia – now Alenia – (Italy) was launched in October 1981, with final assembly by former. ATR 42-200 was basic initial version; ATR 42-300 has same overall dimensions but a higher gross weight, and ATR 42-320 uses PW121 engines for 'hot and high' operations. Freighter version is designated ATR 42F. Stretched-fuselage ATR 74 (see 1991/92 edition) uses same wing but seats up to 72 passengers. Its gross weight is 47,400 lb (21 500 kg) and engines are 2,160 shp (1 611 kW) PW124/2 or (in ATR 72-210) 2,480 shp (1 849 kW) PW127s. Under study in 1992 are 50-seat ATR 52 and 80-seat ATR 82 derivatives.

Dimensions: Span, 80 ft 7½ in (24,57 m); length, 74 ft 4½ in (22,67 m); height, 24 ft 10¾ in (7,59 m); wing area, 586·6 sq ft (54,5 m²).

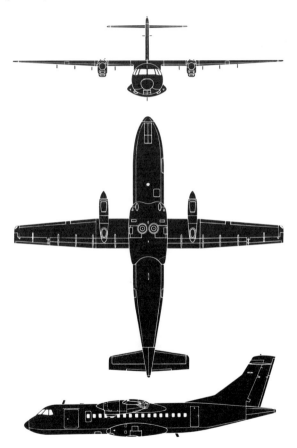

BEECHCRAFT MODEL 1900D

Country of Origin: USA.

Type: Short-haul regional transport.

Power Plant: Two 1,280 shp (955 kW) Pratt & Whitney Canada PT6A-67D turboprops.

Performance: Max cruise speed (at 15,000 lb/6 804 kg), 312 mph (502 km/h) at 10,000 ft (3 050 m), 330 mph (532 km/h) at 25,000 ft (7 620 m); max initial climb (at 16,950 lb/7 688 kg), 2,625 ft/min (13,3 m/sec); service ceiling, 25,000 ft (7 620 m); range (with 19 passengers and IFR reserves), 575 mls (926 km) at 8,000 ft (2 440 m), 656 mls (1 056 km) at 16,000 ft (4 875 m), 794 mls (1 278 km) at 25,000 ft (7 620 m).

Weights: Operational empty, 10,360 lb (4 699 kg); max take-off, 16,950 lb (7 588 kg).

Accommodation: Flight crew of one or two on flight deck and standard cabin arrangement for 19 passengers in single seats on each side of central aisle and three seats against rear bulkhead.

Status: Prototype Model 1900D first flew on 1 March 1990, certification completed March 1991, with initial deliveries (to Mesa Airlines) in November 1991. Mesa order totals 58, for delivery at one a month through 1996. First order for Combi version placed by Mark Air (five), delivery in 1992.

Notes: The Model 1900D is a development of the Model 1900C featuring a deeper fuselage with 28·5 per cent more volume, a flat floor offering stand-up headroom, and larger cabin windows and door. It replaced the Model 1900C in production in October 1991, after 257 of the earlier models built. An Executive 1900D is also available, typically with 12 seats.

BEECHCRAFT MODEL 1900D

Dimensions: Span, 57 ft 10¾ in (17,65 m); length, 57 ft 10 in (17,63 m); height, 14 ft 10⅞ in (4,55 m); wing area, 303 sq ft (28,15 m²).

BEECHCRAFT MODEL 2000A STARSHIP 1

Country of Origin: USA.

Type: Light corporate executive transport.

Power Plant: Two 1,200 shp (895 kW) Pratt & Whitney Canada PT6A-67A turboprops.

Performance: (Model 2000) Max cruise speed, 387 mph (622 km/h) at 25,000 ft (7 620 m), 350 mph (563 km/h) at 35,000 ft (10 670 m); econ cruise, 340 mph (546 km/h) at 35,000 ft (10 670 m); max initial climb, 3,225 ft/min (16,38 m/sec); max range, 1,634 mls (2 629 km) at 35,000 ft (10 670 m).

Weights: Empty equipped, 10,085 lb (4 574 kg); max take-off (Model 2000), 14,500 lb (6 577 kg); max take-off (Model 2000A), 14,900 lb (6 760 kg).

Accommodation: Provision for two crew members on flight deck and standard seating for (Model 2000) eight passengers or (Model 2000A) six passengers.

Status: First of three prototypes flown on 15 February 1986, FAA certification being obtained on 14 June 1988, and first production aircraft flown on 25 April 1989. Fewer than 20 Starships sold by early 1992.

Notes: The Starship, in mating an aft-mounted laminar-flow wing with a variable-sweep foreplane, is highly innovative in concept. Foreplane sweep changes automatically with flap extension to provide pitch-trim compensation. The first pressurised all-composite aircraft to be certificated, the Starship uses such materials as boron, carbon, Kevlar and glassfibre. After building 20 Model 2000s, Beech switched to the Model 2000A in 1992, with higher weight, improved cabin for six instead of eight passengers, more fuel and better payload-range.

BEECHCRAFT MODEL 2000A STARSHIP 1

Dimensions: Span, 54 ft 4¾ in (16,60 m); length, 46 ft 1 in (14,05 m); height, 13 ft 0 in (3,96 m); wing area, 280·9 sq ft (16,09 m²).

BEECHCRAFT T-1A JAYHAWK

Country of Origin: USA.

Type: Tanker/transport flight crew trainer.

Power Plant: Two 2,900 lb st (12·9 kN) Pratt & Whitney Canada JT15D-5B turbofans.

Performance: Max speed, 538 mph (865 km/h) at 41,000 ft (12 495 m); typical cruise, 518 mph (834 km/h) at 41,000 ft (12 495 m); long-range cruise, 455 mph (732 km/h); endurance, over 4 hrs.

Weights: Basic operational, 10,620 lb (4 817 kg); max take-off, 16,100 lb (7 303 kg).

Accommodation: Instructor/observer and two student crew members.

Status: T-1A military version of the Model 400 Beechjet first flown on 5 July 1991, and first deliveries to USAF on 17 January 1992. Deliveries of corporate/executive Model 400 began in June 1986 and first production Model 400A flew on 22 September 1989 with customer deliveries starting November 1990 after FAA certification on 20 June. USAF requirement for T-1A totals 180, with delivery of 27 in 1992, 30 in 1993 and then 36 a year.

Notes: The Model 400 Beechjet originated in Japan as the Mitsubishi Diamond 2, of which 11 were produced. Model 400A was selected by USAF as the basis of its Tanker/Transport Training System (TTTS) on 21 February 1990. Its special features include single-point refuelling, better bird-strike protection and strengthened landing gear. Initial operational capability of the T-1A scheduled for September 1992 at Reese AFB for Air Training Command's Specialised Undergraduate Pilot Training Programme. Japan is buying T-400 transport/trainer developments of the Beechjet 400A, with deliveries to start in 1994.

BEECHCRAFT T-1A JAYHAWK

Dimensions: Span, 43 ft 6 in (13,25 m); length, 48 ft 5 in (14,75 m); height, 13 ft 11 in (4,24 m); wing area, 241·4 sq ft (22,43 m²).

BELL/BOEING V-22 OSPREY

Country of Origin: USA.

Type: Multi-mission tilt-rotor aircraft.

Power Plant: Two 6,150 shp (4 586 kW) Allison T406-AD-400 turboshafts.

Performance: (Manufacturer's estimates) Max cruise speed (aeroplane mode), 316 mph (509 km/h) at sea level, 345 mph (556 km/h) at optimum altitude, (helicopter mode), 115 mph (185 km/h) at sea level; max forward speed with max slung load (15,000 lb/6 804 kg), 230 mph (370 km/h); range (vertical take-off with 12,000-lb/5 443-kg payload), 1,382 mls (2 224 km), (short take-off with 20,000-lb/9 072-kg payload), 2,073 mls (3 336 km); ferry range, 2,418 mls (3 892 km).

Weights: Empty equipped, 34,612 lb (15 700 kg); normal loaded (VTO), 50,705 lb (23 000 kg), (STO), 58,000 lb (26 310 kg).

Accommodation: Normal flight crew of three and up to 24 combat-equipped troops, 12 casualty stretchers plus attendants, or an equivalent cargo load.

Status: First of six prototypes entered flight test on 9 March 1989, and the second on 9 September of that year. Development programme delayed by loss of fifth prototype on 1 June 1991, and, at beginning of 1992, it was proposed that the sixth prototype be completed as a lead-in to production standard aircraft.

Notes: Developed jointly by Bell and Boeing to meet a Joint Services Advanced Vertical Lift Aircraft requirement, the Osprey enjoyed continued development funding early 1992, but no production commitment for this type had been forthcoming.

BELL/BOEING V-22 OSPREY

Dimensions: Span (over rotors), 84 ft 8½ in (25,77 m); length, 62 ft 7⅔ in (19,09 m); height (over tail), 17 ft 7¾ in (5,38 m).

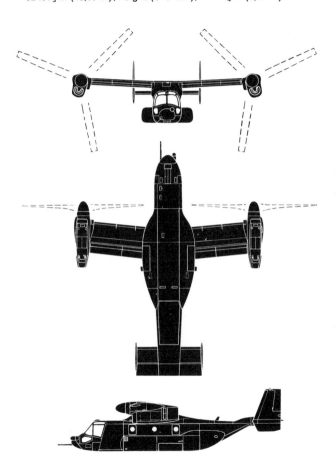

BERIEV BE-42 (MERMAID)

Country of Origin: Commonwealth of Independent States (Russia).

Type: Search and rescue amphibian flying boat.

Power Plant: Two 33,070 lb st (147·1 kN) MKB (Soloviev) D-30KPV turbofans and provision for two 6,173 lb st (27·5 kN) Rybinsk Novikov RKBM RD-36-35 auxiliary turbojets.

Performance: Max speed, 497 mph (800 km/h); max continuous cruise, 435 mph (700 km/h); econ cruise, 342 mph (550 km/h); service ceiling, 42,650 ft (13 000 m); range (with 14,330 lb/6 500 kg payload), 2,880 mls (4 635 km); max range, 3,455 mls (5 560 km).

Weights: Max loaded, 189,595 lb (86 000 kg).

Status: First of two prototypes of the Be-40 (alias A-40) Albatross was flown in April 1987, the second prototype being modified for search and rescue tasks as the Be-42. Series production of the Be-40 at Taganrog against initial order for 20 was expected to commence during 1992.

Accommodation: Flight crew of three-five plus rescue team of four-six (with power boats, life rafts and other specialised equipment) and provision for up to 54 survivors.

Notes: Conceived primarily for anti-submarine warfare and surveillance as the Be-40 (alias A-40), the Beriev amphibian has been developed for the dedicated ASR task under the designation Be-42. Proposed versions include a water bomber capable of lifting a 25-*tonne* water load, a 95-to-100-passenger transport, the Be-40P, and a combination freighter and passenger transport, the Be-40PT, capable of carrying a 6,5-*tonne* freight load plus up to 37 passengers over 3,107 mls (5 000 km). Provision is made for auxiliary turbojets (mounted below the primary turbofans) to improve water take-off performance when necessary.

BERIEV BE-42 (MERMAID)

Dimensions: Span, 137 ft 9½ in (42,00 m); length, 137 ft 9½ in (42,00 m); height, 36 ft 1 in (11,00 m).

BOEING 737-300

Country of Origin: USA.

Type: Short-to-medium-range jet transport.

Power Plant: Two 20,000 lb st (89 kN) CFM56-3B1 or 22,000 lb st (97,9 kN) CFM56-3B2 turbofans.

Performance: Max cruise speed, 565 mph (908 km/h) at 26,000 ft (7 925 m); range cruise, 494 mph (794 km/h) at 35,000 ft (10 670 m); range with 128 passengers and standard fuel, 2,090 mls (3 362 km); range with 128 passengers and max fuel, 3,090 mls (4 973 km).

Weights: Operational empty, 69,580 lb (31 561 kg); max take-off, 124,500–138,500 lb (56 473–62 882 kg).

Accommodation: Flight crew of two and up to 149 (-300) or 132 (-500) passengers six abreast with single aisle at 30-in (76-cm) pitch; typical mixed-class layout (-300) for eight first class and 120 tourist.

Status: Development and production go-ahead for -300 on 26 March 1981. Flight test aircraft first flown on 24 February, 2 March and 2 May 1984. FAA certification 14 November 1984, first deliveries 28 November (US Air) and 30 November (Southwest), first revenue service (Southwest), 7 December 1984. Total sales, Srs 300,928; Srs 400,348; Srs 500,260. Overall total sales of -300/-400/-500 includes 269 unspecified by variant. Total Boeing 737 family sales, 2,957 by early 1992.

Notes: The -300/-400/-500 variants feature CFM56 engines and vary in fuselage lengths and passenger capacities. The -400 has a length of 119 ft 7 in (36,45 m) and can carry up to 188 passengers or 146 in typical two-class layout. The -500 is 101 ft 9 in (31,01 m) long and seats 108 in two classes or a maximum of 132.

Dimensions: Span, 94 ft 9 in (28,88 m); length, 109 ft 7 in (33,40 m); height, 36 ft 6 in (11,13 m); wing area, 1,135 sq ft (105,4 m²).

BOEING 747-400

Country of Origin: USA.

Type: Long-haul commercial transport.

Power Plant: (Options) Four 57,900 lb st (257·5 kN) General Electric CF6-80C2B4, 56,750 lb st (252·39 kN) Pratt & Whitney PW4256, or 58,000 lb st (258 kN) Rolls-Royce RB211-524G turbofans.

Performance: (RB211) Max speed, 606 mph (976 km/h) at 30,000 ft (9 150 m); max cruise, 583 mph (939 km/h) at 35,000 ft (10 670 m); range cruise, 564 mph (907 km/h); range (412 passengers and typical reserves), 8,406 mls (13 528 km).

Weights: (RB211) Operational empty, 393,880 lb (178 661 kg); max take-off (options), 800,000 lb (362 875 kg), 850,000 lb (385 555 kg), or 870,000 lb (394 625 kg).

Accommodation: Flight crew of two and typical three-class seating for 450 passengers with maximum of 660 passengers.

Status: First 747-400 flown on 29 April 1988, with customer deliveries (to Northwest Orient) commencing on 26 January 1989. Total of 444 -400s on firm order by beginning of 1991, these following 205 -100s, 383 -200s and 80 -300s, as well as 43 of the short-body 747 SPs and 15 assorted versions for non-commercial users. Total 747 sales, 1,170.

Notes: The current production version of the Boeing 747, the -400, differs in a number of respects from the preceding -300 which incorporated structural changes to the upper deck area increasing upper deck accommodation to 69 (economy class) passengers. The most significant external changes of the -400 are an extended wing and vertical winglets although a few 747-400s lack the last-mentioned feature. A Combi cargo/passenger version is designated 747-400M and an all-cargo version is designated 747-400F.

BOEING 747-400

Dimensions: Span, 211 ft 0 in (64,31 m); length, 231 ft $10\frac{1}{4}$ in (70,67 m); height, 63 ft 4 in (19,30 m); wing area, 5,650 sq ft (524,88 m²).

BOEING 757-200

Country of origin: USA.

Type: Short- to medium-haul commercial transport.

Power Plant: (Options) Two 37,400 lb st (166·4 kN) Rolls-Royce RB211-535C or 40,100 lb st (178·4 kN) -535E4, 38,200 lb st (170 kN) Pratt & Whitney PW2037 or 41,700 lb st (185·5 kN) PW2040 turbofans.

Performance: (RB211-535E4) Max cruise speed, 570 mph (917 km/h) at 30,000 ft (9 145 m); econ cruise, 528 mph (850 km/h) at 39,000 ft (11 885 m); range (with max payload), 3,660 mls (5 890 km), (max fuel), 5,257 mls (8 460 km).

Weights: Operational empty, 126,060 lb (57 180 kg); max take-off (medium range), 230,000 lb (104 325 kg), (long range), 250,000 lb (113 395 kg).

Accommodation: Flight crew of two and nine standard interior arrangements for 178 (16 first and 162 tourist class), 186 (16 first and 170 tourist class), 202 (12 first and 190 tourist class), 208 (12 first and 196 tourist class), or 214, 220, 223, 224 or 239 tourist class passengers.

Status: First Model 757 flown 19 February 1982, with first customer deliveries (to Eastern) on 22 December 1982. Total orders and options for 785 at the beginning of 1992 with more than 400 delivered and production continuing at seven monthly.

Notes: Current variants of the basic Boeing 757 include the 757-200PF (Package Freighter) featuring a large side cargo door in the forward fuselage and a windowless interior (photo above), and the 757-200M Combi, which, retaining all passenger windows, has an upward-opening cargo door in the forward fuselage. EROPS (Extended Range Operations) FAA approval over water has been granted with both Rolls-Royce and Pratt & Whitney engines.

Dimensions: Span, 124 ft 10 in (38,05 m); length, 155 ft 3 in (47,32 m); height, 44 ft 6 in (13,56 m); wing area, 1,994 sq ft (185,25 m²).

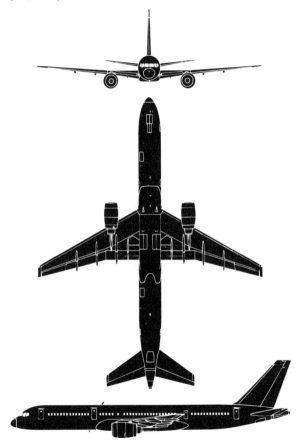

BOEING 767-300

Country of Origin: USA.

Type: Medium-haul commercial transport.

Power Plant: Two 50,000 lb st (222·4 kN) Pratt & Whitney PW4050 or 52,000 lb st (231·3 kN) PW4052, or 52,500 lb st (233·5 kN) General Electric CF6-80C2B2 turbofans.

Performance: (CF6-80C2B2) Max cruise speed (at 260,000 lb/ 117 935 kg), 563 mph (906 km/h) at 39,000 ft (11 890 m); range cruise, 529 mph (852 km/h) at 39,000 ft (11 890 m); range (max payload), 3,706 mls (5 965 km), (max fuel) 6,160 mls (9 915 km).

Weights: Operational empty, 191,700 lb (86 953 kg); max take-off, 345,000 lb (156 489 kg).

Accommodation: Flight crew of two and basic arrangement for 216 passengers comprising 18 first-class six abreast and 198 tourist-class seven abreast. Alternative single-class layouts for 230, 242 and 255 passengers.

Status: First Model 767 flown on 26 September 1981, with first customer delivery (United) following 19 August 1982. First -300 flown on 30 January 1986, with first delivery (JAL) following 25 September. Orders and options (all versions) totalled 598 aircraft at the beginning of 1992, with approximately 405 delivered and production continuing at a rate of five monthly.

Notes: The -300 version of the Boeing 767 differs from the -200 primarily in having a 21·25-ft (6,48-m) fuselage stretch, a strengthened undercarriage and increased-gauge skinning in some areas. Variants include the -300ER extended-range model with optional gross weights of up to 400,000 lb (181 439 kg), and the necessary structural changes to accommodate these and increased fuel capacity. An AEW version of the 767, with dorsal rotodome, is under consideration in 1992.

Dimensions: Span, 156 ft 1 in (47,57 m); length, 180 ft 3 in (54,94 m); height, 52 ft 0 in (15,85 m); wing area, 3,050 sq ft (283,3 m²).

BOEING E-3 SENTRY

Country of Origin: USA.

Type: Airborne warning and control system aircraft.

Power Plant: Four (E-3A, B and C) 21,000 lb st (93·4 kN) Pratt & Whitney TF33-PW-100/100A or (E-3D and F) 24,000 lb st (106·76 kN) CFM International CFM56-2A-3 turbofans.

Performance: (E-3A, B and C) Max speed, 530 mph (853 km/h) at 30,000 ft (9 145 m); max continuous cruise, 495 mph (797 km/h) at 29,000 ft (8 840 m); typical loiter speed, 376 mph (605 km/h); max unrefuelled endurance, 11·5 hrs; time on station at 1,000 mls (1 610 km) from base, 6 hrs; ferry range, 5,034 mls (8 100 km) at 475 mph (764 km/h).

Weights: (E-3A) Empty, 170,277 lb (77 238 kg); normal loaded, 214,300 lb (97 206 kg); max take-off, 325,000 lb (147 420 kg).

Accommodation: Basic flight crew of four on flight deck and normal mission crew of 13 systems operators occupying tactical compartments (this number can vary for specific missions).

Status: First of two development aircraft flown 9 February 1972, these and 22 E-3As built for USAF subsequently being updated to E-3B standard and redelivered from July 1984. Final 10 for USAF (including updated third test aircraft) delivered as E-3Cs. Eighteen E-3As (similar in standard to E-3C) delivered to multi-national NATO force 1982–1985. All subsequent Sentries powered by CFM56 engines, these comprising five for Royal Saudi Air Force delivered 1986–87, seven (E-3Ds) for the RAF with last delivered 1992, and four (E-3Fs) for France's *Armée de l'Air* with deliveries completed 1991.

Notes: The E-3D Sentry AEW Mk 1 for the RAF (illustrated) features additional outboard wing stringers and stiffeners to cater for tip pods and trailing-edge HF antennae. The final E-3D was also the last airframe of the Boeing 707 family built.

BOEING E-3 SENTRY

Dimensions: (E-3D) Span, 147 ft 7 in (44,98 m); length, 152 ft 11 in (46,61 m); height, 41 ft 9 in (12,73 m); wing area, 2,892 sq ft (268,67 m²).

BRITISH AEROSPACE 125

Country of Origin: United Kingdom.

Type: Corporate transport and military multi-role aircraft.

Power Plant: Two 4,300 lb st (19,13 kN) Garrett TFE731-5R-1H turbofans.

Performance: Max cruise speed, 525 mph (845 km/h) at 29,000 ft (8 840 m); econ cruise, 461 mph (741 km/h) at 39,000–43,000 ft (11 900–13 100 m); max initial climb, 3,100 ft/min (15,7 m/sec); service ceiling, 43,000 ft (13 100 m); range (max payload), 3,305 mls (5 318 km); (max fuel with VFR reserves, 3,454 mls (5 560 km).

Weights: Operational empty, 15,120 lb (6 858 km); max take-off, 27,400 lb (12 430 kg).

Accommodation: Flight crew of two (with provision for third crew member on flight deck) and (typically) two individual chairs, a three-seat settee and club-four seating for nine passengers. Max 14 seats in cabin.

Status: Prototype D.H.125 (progenitor of the family) flown on 13 August 1962. Total sales of original Viper-engined variants, 358. First Srs 700, with TFE731 engines, flown 29 June 1976, and production totalled 215. First Srs 800 flown 26 May 1983, sales to early 1992, 220. Production rate in 1992, four aircraft per month (Srs 800 and Srs 1000 combined).

Notes: The BAe 125 Srs 800 is one of two variants of the 125 continuing in production in 1992 – see separate description of BAe 1000. As well as serving in its primary rôle of executive transport, the Srs 800 has been adopted as an ambulance (Swiss Air Ambulance Service), for flight calibration (by USAF as the C-29A, and by JASDF) and for search-and-rescue (by JASDF, requiring 27 U-125As for delivery 1995–2003). Proposed military versions include the P.134 for SIGINT and P.135 for radar reconnaissance.

Dimensions: Span, 51 ft 4½ in (15,66 m); length, 51 ft 2 in (15,60 m); height, 17 ft 7 in (5,36 m); wing area, 374 sq ft (34,75 m²).

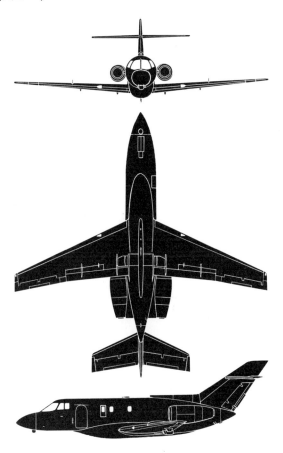

BRITISH AEROSPACE RJ70/80

Country of Origin: United Kingdom.
Type: Short-haul regional airliner.
Power Plant: Four 6,130 lb st (27·3 kN) (derated) Textron Lycoming LF507 turbofans.
Performance: Max cruise speed (for 575-ml/925-km sector), 477 mph (767 km/h) at 29,000 ft (8 840 m); range cruise, 416 mph (669 km/h); range (RJ70), 920 mls (1 480 km) with 70 passengers and reserves, (RJ80), 980 mls (1 575 km) with 80 passengers and reserves.
Weights: Operational empty, 23,500 lb (10 660 kg); max take-off (RJ70), 80,000 lb (32 288 kg), (RJ80), 84,000 lb (38 100 kg).
Accommodation: Flight crew of two and seating (typical) for (RJ70) 70 passengers five abreast, or (RJ80) 80 passengers six abreast.
Status: RJ70 concept aircraft (modified BAe 146-100) demonstrated from autumn 1990, with first series model to fly July 1992 and first deliveries in mid-1993 to launch customer Business Express, which ordered 20 in December 1991.
Notes: The RJ70 and RJ80, respectively aimed at the North American and European markets, are derivatives of the BAe 146 Series 100 optimised for the regional jet transport market. Differing primarily in cabin arrangments, both RJ70 and RJ80 have the LF507 turbofan, which became available from late 1991 and offers increased thrust at higher temperatures. It is derated from 7,000 lb st (31·13 kN) for installation in these commuter aircraft to afford improved life and economy. Lightweight versions of the basic BAe 146 Srs 100, the RJ70 and RJ80 are designed to operate at weights related to the shorter ranges and higher frequency of landings that are found in typical regional/commuter networks.

BRITISH AEROSPACE RJ70/80

Dimensions: Span, 86 ft 0 in (26,21 m); length, 85 ft $11\frac{1}{2}$ in (26,20 m); height, 28 ft 3 in (8,61 m); wing area, 832 sq ft (77,30 m²).

BRITISH AEROSPACE 146-300

Country of Origin: United Kingdom.
Type: Short-haul commercial transport.
Power Plant: Four 7,000 lb st (31·13 kN) Textron Lycoming LF507 turbofans.
Performance: (ALF502R-5 engines) Max cruise speed, 494 mph (795 km/h) at 26,000 ft (7 925 m); long-range cruise, 434 mph (699 km/h) at 29,000 ft (8 840 m); range (standard fuel), 1,750 mls (2 817 km), (max payload), 1,197 mls (1 927 km).
Weights: Operational empty, 56,185 lb (25 485 kg); max take-off, 97,500 lb (44 225 kg); optional high gross weight, 101,500 lb (46 040 kg).
Accommodation: Flight crew of two and standard seating for 103 passengers five abreast and a maximum of 128.
Status: Aerodynamic prototype of 146-300 (conversion of first 146-100 prototype) flown on 1 May 1987, with first production Series 300 following in June 1988. First flight (LF507 engines) 2 March 1991. Orders totalled 52 (including eight -300QTs) by beginning of 1992 when sales of all versions totalled 222, of which about 190 delivered.
Notes: The BAe 146 Series 300 represents the second 'stretch' of the basic design, possessing the same wing and engines as the Series 100 and 200 but a still longer fuselage. All three Series are available in QT (Quiet Trader) dedicated freighter form and QC quick-change convertible passenger/freighter form. From mid-1992, all versions are available in 'New Generation' configuration, powered by LF507 turbofans in place of the original 6,970 lb st (31,0 kN) ALF502R-5 engines. The updating allows a 4,000-lb (1 815-kg) increase in the gross weight of the Series 300, a greater payload and a 173-ml (278-km) max payload range increase.

BRITISH AEROSPACE 146-300

Dimensions: Span, 86 ft 0 in (26,21 m); length, 101 ft 8 in (30,99 m); height, 28 ft 3 in (8,61 m); wing area, 832 sq ft (77,30 m²).

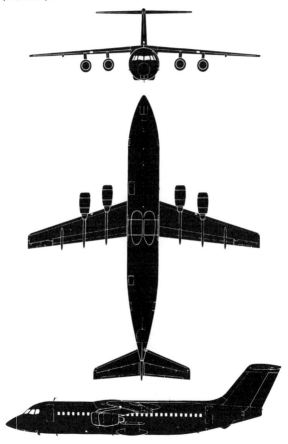

BRITISH AEROSPACE 1000

Country of Origin: United Kingdom.
Type: Corporate executive transport.
Power Plant: Two 5,200 lb st (23·13 kN) Pratt & Whitney Canada PW305 turbofans.
Performance: Max cruise speed, 539 mph (867 km/h) at 29,000 ft (8 840 m); econ cruise, 463 mph (745 km/h) at 39,000–43,000 ft (11 890–13 100 m); time to 35,000 ft (10 670 m), 22 min; service ceiling, 43,000 ft (13 100 m); range (max payload), 3,960 mls (6 375 km), (max fuel with VFR reserves), 4,185 mls (6 736 km).
Weights: Empty, 16,820 lb (7 629 kg); max take-off, 31,000 lb (14 060 kg).
Accommodation: Flight crew of two (with provision for third crew member on flight deck) and (typically) eight passengers in a double 'club-four' arrangement, or one 'club-four' plus three-seat divan and one single seat in main cabin. Up to 15 passengers in 'business express' configuration.
Status: First of two development aircraft flown on 16 June 1990, with second following on 26 November. These were joined early in 1991 by first series aircraft, which contributed to the 800-hr flight development programme for certification, obtained in UK on 21 October 1991. US certification followed on 31 October. Orders and commitments for 22 BAe 1000s had been received by the beginning of 1992.
Notes: A long-range, larger-cabin derivative of the BAe 125 (which remains in production in its Srs 800 form), the BAe 1000 features a 2 ft 9 in (0,84-m) fuselage stretch, new and more powerful engines, a fuel tank in an extended forward wing fairing and increased ventral tank capacity. The re-styled cabin interior offers increased headroom.

Dimensions: Span, 51 ft 4½ in (15,66 m); length, 53 ft 10½ in (16,42 m); height, 17 ft 1 in (5,21 m); wing area, 374 sq ft (34,75 m²).

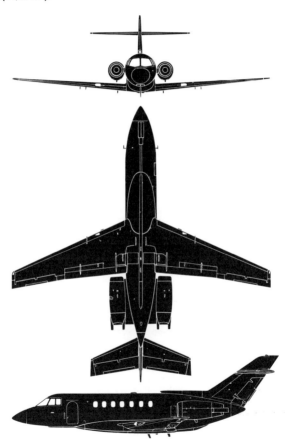

BRITISH AEROSPACE ATP

Country of Origin: United Kingdom.
Type: Regional commercial transport.
Power Plant: Two 2,653 shp (1 978 kW) Pratt & Whitney Canada PW126A turboprops.
Performance: Max cruise speed, 306 mph (493 km/h) at 13,000 ft (3 960 m); econ cruise, 272 mph (437 km/h) at 18,000 ft (5 485 m); range (max payload with reserves), 390 mls (630 km), (with 68 passengers and reserves), 921 mls (1,482 km).
Weights: Operational empty, 31,290 lb (14 193 kg); max take-off, 50,550 lb (22 930 kg).
Accommodation: Flight crew of two and standard arrangement for 64 passengers four abreast with central aisle, and alternative arrangements for 60 to 72 seats.
Status: Two prototypes flown on 6 August 1986 and 20 February 1987, with certification following in March 1988. The first revenue service was flown (by British Midland) on 9 March 1988. By early 1992, orders for the ATP from nine operators totalled 59 aircraft, plus additional options.
Notes: The ATP (Advanced TurboProp) is technically a stretched development of the BAe (originally Avro) 748, with new engines, systems and equipment, slightly swept-back fin and rudder and redesigned fuselage nose. It incorporates an advanced flight deck with EFIS (Electronic Flight Instrument System) and extensively modernised and improved interior. An anti-submarine warfare/anti-surface vessel warfare (ASW/ASVW) derivative of the ATP is proposed as the P132, but no sales had been recorded for this version up to April 1992.

BRITISH AEROSPACE ATP

Dimensions: Span, 100 ft 6 in (30,63 m); length, 85 ft 4 in (26,01 m); height, 24 ft 11 in (7,59 m); wing area, 842·84 sq ft (78,30 m²).

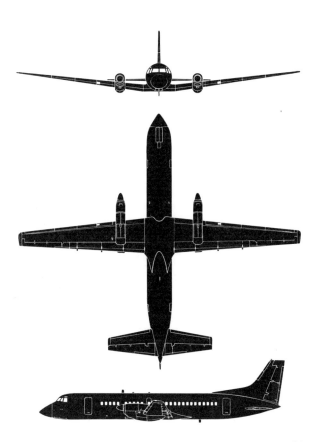

BRITISH AEROSPACE HARRIER GR MK 7

Countries of Origin: United Kingdom and USA.

Type: Single-seat V/STOL close support and tactical reconnaissance aircraft.

Power Plant: One 21,750 lb st (96·75 kN) Rolls-Royce Pegasus Mk 105 vectored-thrust turbofan.

Performance: Max speed, 661 mph (1 065 km/h) at sea level, or Mach=0·87, 600 mph (966 km/h) at 36,000 ft (10 975 m), or Mach=0·91; tactical radius (with one hour loiter and 12 Mk 82 bombs), 103 mls (167 km), (HI-LO-HI mission profile with seven Mk 82 bombs and two 250 Imp gal/1 136 l external tanks, but no loiter allowance), 553 mls (889 km); ferry range (max external fuel), 2,015 mls (3 243 km) tanks retained.

Weights: Operational empty (including pilot), approx 14,000 lb (6 350 kg); max take-off (VTO), 18,950 lb (8 595 kg), (STO), 31,000 lb (14 061 kg).

Armament: Two 25-mm cannon (on under-fuselage stations) and up to 16 Mk 82 or six Mk 83 bombs, six BL-755 cluster bombs, four Maverick ASMs, or 10 rocket pods on six wing stations. Max external load, 9,200 lb (4 173 kg).

Status: First Harrier GR Mk 7 (converted GR Mk 5) flown 29 November 1989, followed by second conversion, with first production aircraft flying May 1990 and first delivery on following 12 September. Delivery of new-build aircraft paralleled upgrading to similar standard of 18 GR Mk 5As (interim upgrade of GR Mk 5), to be followed by upgrade of 42 GR Mk 5s to full GR Mk 7 standard.

Notes: Based on the Harrier GR Mk 5 (the RAF equivalent of the US Marine Corps' AV-8B), the GR Mk 7 has additional equipment for nocturnal and bad weather operations. The GR Mk 7 airframe is built jointly by British Aerospace and McDonnell Douglas on a 50-50 basis. See TAV-8B, pages 158–9.

BRITISH AEROSPACE HARRIER GR MK 7

Dimensions: Span, 30 ft 4 in (9,24 m); length, 46 ft 4 in (14,12 m); height, 11 ft 7¾ in (3,55 m); wing area (including LERX), 238·7 sq ft (22,18 m²).

BRITISH AEROSPACE HAWK 100

Country of Origin: United Kingdom.

Type: Tandem two-seat advanced systems trainer and light ground attack aircraft.

Power Plant: One 5,845 lb st (26·0 kN) Rolls-Royce Turboméca Adour 871 turbofan.

Performance: Max speed, 644 mph (1 037 km/h) at sea level, or Mach = 0·845, 580 mph (933 km/h) at 36,000 ft (10 975 m), or Mach = 0·88; max initial climb, 11,800 ft/min (59,95 m/sec); combat radius (with four 1,000-lb/453,6-kg bombs and gun pod), 148 mls (239 km) LO-LO-LO, 759 mls (1 222 km) HI-LO-HI; endurance combat air patrol (with two AAMs, a 30-mm gun pod and two 190 Imp gal/864 l drop tanks), 2·75 hrs.

Weights: Empty, 8,752 lb (3 970 kg); max take-off, 18,739 lb (8 500 kg).

Armament: One 30-mm cannon pod on fuselage centreline and up to six Sidewinder AAMs (four underwing and two at wingtips), or (ground attack) four 1,000-lb (453,6-kg) or eight 500-lb (226,8-kg) bombs.

Status: Aerodynamic prototype (modified from Hawk 60 demonstrator) flown 21 October 1987, with second (fully representative) prototype joining the flight test programme in 1990. First production aircraft completed as demonstrator (Hawk 102D) flown 29 February 1992, and first customer delivery scheduled for September 1992, this being first of 18 Hawk 102s for Abu Dhabi. Other orders at beginning of 1992 included four Hawk 103s for Oman and 10 Hawk 108s for Malaysia. Brunei had announced its intention of procuring eight.

Notes: An upgraded development of the Hawk basic/advanced trainer which remains in production in its Hawk 60 series, the Hawk 100 features a 'combat wing' with manually-selected combat flap and fixed leading-edge droop.

Dimensions: Span (over wingtip AAMs), 32 ft 7⅜ in (9,94 m); length (excluding probe), 38 ft 4 in (11,68 m); height, 13 ft 8 in (4,16 m); wing area, 179·6 sq ft (16,69 m²).

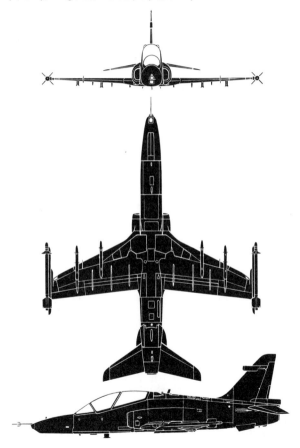

BRITISH AEROSPACE HAWK 200

Country of Origin: United Kingdom.
Type: Single-seat multi-role lightweight fighter.
Power Plant: One 5,845 lb st (26·0 kN) Rolls-Royce Turboméca Adour 871 turbofan.
Performance: Max speed, 634 mph (1 021 km/h) at sea level, or Mach=0·83; econ cruise, 495 mph (796 km/h) at 41,000 ft (12 500 m); max initial climb, 11,510 ft/min (58,47 m/sec); range (internal fuel), 554 mls (892 km), (with one 130 and two 190 Imp gal/592 and 864 l external tanks), 2,244 mls (3 610 km).
Weights: Empty, 9,943 lb (4 510 kg); max take-off, 20,065 lb (9 101 kg).
Armament: One or two internally-mounted 25-mm Aden cannon and up to five Sidewinder AAMs, or (close air support) up to five 1,000-lb (453,6-kg) and four 500-lb (226,8-kg) bombs. Each wing pylon capable of lifting 2,000 lb (907 kg) within a maximum external ordnance load of 7,700 lb (3 493 kg).
Status: First prototype flown on 19 May 1986, with first pre-production aircraft following on 24 April 1987, and demonstrator (Hawk 200RDA) with Westinghouse APG-66H multi-mode radar flown 13 February 1992. Production deliveries scheduled to commence mid-1994 with eight (Hawk 203s) to Oman and 18 (Hawk 208s) to Malaysia. Both Brunei and Saudi Arabia (Hawk 205) had announced their intention of procuring this type at the beginning of 1992.
Notes: Originally evolved as a private venture single-seat combat version of the Hawk trainer, the Hawk 200 series is virtually identical with the two-seat Hawk 100 series aft of the cockpit, giving 80 per cent airframe commonality. The 'combat wing' is similar to that of the Hawk 100 series which may also have a similar avionics fit.

Dimensions: Span (over wingtip AAMs), 32 ft 7⅜ in (9,94 m); length, 37 ft 4 in (11,38 m); height, 13 ft 8 in (4,16 m); wing area, 179·6 sq ft (16,69 m²).

BRITISH AEROSPACE JETSTREAM 41

Country of Origin: United Kingdom.
Type: Light regional commercial transport.
Power Plant: Two 1,500 shp (1 118 kW) Garrett TPE331-14GR/HR turboprops.
Performance: (Estimated) Max cruise speed, 336 mph (541 km/h) at 20,000 ft (6 100 m); econ cruise, 299 mph (482 km/h) at 20,000 ft (6 100 m); max initial climb, 2,200 ft/min (11,18 m/sec); service ceiling, 26,000 ft (7 925 m); range (29 passengers and IFR reserves), 680 mls (1 095 km).
Weights: Operational empty (typical), 13,544 lb (6 144 kg); max take-off, 22,377 lb (10 150 kg).
Accommodation: Flight crew of two and up to 29 or (with galley) 27 passengers three abreast.
Status: First of three aircraft for flight development (to be delivered to customers subsequently) flown on 25 September 1991, with customer deliveries to commence in the fourth quarter of 1992. Second aircraft flown on 6 February 1992 for 'hot and high' testing with third on 27 March for EFIS trials. Commitments for 115 Jetstream 41s recorded by early 1992.
Notes: The Jetstream 41 was derived from the Jetstream Super 31, from which it differs primarily in having a lengthened fuselage with improved cabin access, and a longer-span wing mounted lower on the fuselage to avoid wing carry-through structure interrupting the cabin. A rearward-extended wing-root fairing provides additional baggage space. More than 400 Jetstream 31s and Super 31s had been ordered from British Aerospace by early 1992, and further derivatives of the basic design were under consideration.

Dimensions: Span, 60 ft 0 in (18,29 m); length, 63 ft 2 in (19,25 m); height, 18 ft 10 in (5,74 m); wing area, 350·8 sq ft (32,59 m²).

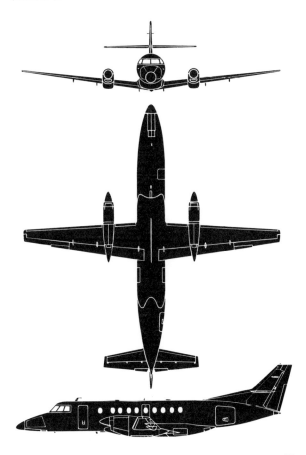

BRITISH AEROSPACE SEA HARRIER
FRS MK 2

Country of Origin: United Kingdom.

Type: Single-seat V/STOL shipboard multi-role fighter.

Power Plant: One 21,500 lb st (95·6 kN) Rolls-Royce Pegasus 106 vectored-thrust turbofan.

Performance: Max speed, 720 mph (1 160 km/h) at 1,000 ft (305 m), or Mach=0·95, 607 mph (977 km/h) at 36,000 ft (10 975 m), or Mach=0·92, (with two Martel ASMs and two AIM-9L AAMs), 598 mph (962 km/h) at sea level, or Mach= 0·83; combat radius (high altitude intercept with 3 min combat) 480 mls (750 km), (surface attack with two Sea Eagle AShMs and two 30-mm cannon), 230 mls (370 km).

Weights: Approx operational empty, 14,500 lb (6 577 kg); max take-off, 26,500 lb (12 020 kg).

Armament: External fuselage packs for two 30-mm cannon, or two AIM-20 AAMs on fuselage stations, plus two stores stations under each wing for free-fall or retarded 1,000-lb (453,6-kg) bombs, cluster bombs, 68-mm rocket packs, AIM-9L or AIM-120 AAMs, Sea Eagle AShMs, or ALARM anti-radiation missiles.

Status: The first of two development Sea Harrier FRS Mk 2s (converted from FRS Mk 1s) was flown on 19 September 1988. Contract for conversion of further 33 FRS Mk 1s to FRS Mk 2 standard 7 December 1988, with redelivery from 1992 and continuing into 1996. An order for 10 new-build FRS Mk 2s for the Royal Navy placed March 1990.

Notes: The Sea Harrier FRS Mk 2 differs from the FRS Mk 1 which it begins to supplant in 1992 by having a Blue Vixen pulse-Doppler radar in place of the Blue Fox and enabling all-weather look-down detection with track-while-scan, multiple-target-engagement capability. It features a redesigned cockpit, a lengthened aft fuselage, upgraded systems and the ability to carry up to four AIM-120 fire-and-forget medium-range AAMs.

Dimensions: Span, 25 ft 3 in (7,70 m); length, 46 ft 6 in (14,17 m); height, 12 ft 2 in (3,71 m).

CANADAIR CL-415

Country of Origin: Canada.
Type: Multi-purpose amphibian.
Power Plant: Two 2,380 shp (1 775 kW) Pratt & Whitney Canada PW123AF turboprops.
Performance: Max cruise speed (at 32,500 lb/14 741 kg), 227 mph (365 km/h) at 5,000 ft (1 525 m); range cruise, 178 mph (287 km/h); max initial climb (at 46,000 lb/20 865 kg), 1,375 ft/min (7,0 m/sec); ferry range, 1,508 mls (2 427 km).
Weights: Operational empty (utility), 25,990 lb (11 789 kg), (water bomber), 27,190 lb (12 333 kg); max take-off (land), 43,850 lb (19 890 kg), (water) 37,700 lb (17 100 kg); max flying weight (after water scooping), 46,000 lb (20 865 kg).
Accommodation: Normal flight crew of two with additional stations for flight engineer, navigator and two observers for maritime surveillance duties, or 32–35 passengers in transport configuration. Maximum disposable payload of 13,500 lb (6 123 kg) as a water bomber or 10,560 lb (4 790 kg) utility.
Status: Two CL-215T prototypes (converted from CL-215s) were flown on 8 June and 20 September 1989. Delivery of 15 CL-215T conversions to Spain began on 5 June 1991. Two prototypes returned to Quebec's SAG on 29 January and in February 1992. CL-415 production launched on 16 October 1991 based on orders/commitments from the French *Sécurité Civile* for 12 and Quebec's SAG for eight.
Notes: CL-415 designation applies to new-build aircraft, similar to CL-215T conversions (as in photo above) of original piston-engined CL-215 (of which 125 built, last delivery May 1990). Exclusive to the CL-415 are a four-door drop system with larger water tanks, fully-powered flight controls and improved cockpit with EFIS.

CANADAIR CL-415

Dimensions: Span, 93 ft 10 in (28,60 m); length, 65 ft 0¼ in (19,82 m); height (on land), 29 ft 5½ in (8,98 m); wing area, 1,080 sq ft (100,33 m²).

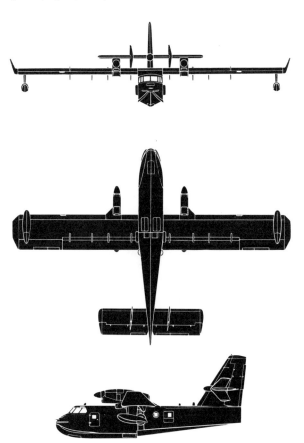

CANADAIR REGIONAL JET

Country of Origin: Canada.

Type: Regional transport.

Power Plant: Two 8,729 lb st (38·83 kN) or 9,220 lb st (41·0 kN) (with automatic power reserve) General Electric CF34-3AI turbofans.

Performance: (Manufacturer's estimates) Max cruise speed, 528 mph (850 km/h) at 36,000 ft (10 975 m), or Mach = 0·80; long-range cruise, 488 mph (786 km/h) at 36,000 ft (10 975 m), or Mach = 0·74; max initial climb, 3,500 ft/min (17,8 m/sec); time to 35,000 ft (10 670 m), 23 min; range (max payload), 972 mls (1 564 km); extended range option, 1,651 mls (2 659 km).

Weights: Operational empty, 30,100 lb (13 653 kg); max take-off, 47,450 lb (21 523 kg), or (ER option), 51,000 lb (23 133 kg).

Accommodation: Flight crew of two and standard cabin layout for 50 passengers four abreast.

Status: First two test aircraft flown on 10 May and 2 August 1991; third, fully-furnished, aircraft flown on 17 November 1991. Initial customer deliveries (to Lufthansa City Line) in third quarter of 1992. By the beginning of 1992, firm orders totalled 35, plus 36 options, from three airlines, memoranda of agreements for more than 60, and the first Corporate RJ (a Series 100-ER), to be delivered to Xerox Corp in December 1992.

Notes: The Regional Jet, or RJ, is a derivative of the Challenger (over 250 sold) embodying fuselage extensions of 10 ft 8 in (3,25 m) forward of the wing and 9 ft 4 in (2,84 m) aft, an increase of some 15 per cent in wing area, and various other changes to translate the aircraft from light corporate executive transport to regional airliner. The basic 50-seater is the Series 100 and the extended-range model is the Series 100-ER. The Series 200, with a lengthened fuselage, is under study.

CANADAIR REGIONAL JET

Dimensions: Span, 70 ft 4 in (21,44 m); length, 88 ft 5 in (26,95 m); height, 20 ft 8 in (6,30 m); wing area, 520·4 sq ft (48,35 m²).

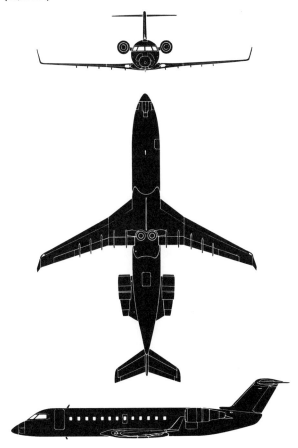

CESSNA MODEL 525 CITATIONJET

Country of Origin: USA.

Type: Light corporate executive transport.

Power Plant: Two 1,900 lb st (8·45 kN) Williams International FJ44 turbojets.

Performance: (Manufacturer's estimates) Max cruise, 437 mph (703 km/h) at 35,000 ft (10 670 m); max initial climb, 3,540 ft/min (18 m/sec); max certificated altitude, 41,000 ft (12 495 m); range (max payload, IFR reserves), 1,238 mls (1 992 km); range (max fuel, IFR reserves), 1,490 mls (2 400 km).

Weights: Empty, 5,730 lb (2 599 kg); max take-off, 10,000 lb (4 536 kg).

Accommodation: Pilot and co-pilot/passenger on flight deck and standard main cabin arrangement for five passengers in two forward- and two aft-facing seats, and one side-facing seat.

Status: First prototype flown 29 April 1991, followed by pre-production prototype (for eventual customer sale) on 20 November 1991. FAA certification completed in December 1991, with customer deliveries commencing at the beginning of 1992. Production planning provides for 50 CitationJets in 1993 and 80 in 1994, against backlog exceeding 100 by early 1992.

Notes: Intended successor to the Citation I, production of which terminated in 1985, the CitationJet retains the forward fuselage structure of the Citation II, which is combined with a new 'natural laminar flow' (NLF) wing, new rear fuselage and a T-type tail. Production of the original Model 500 Citation totalled 349, and of the Citation I, 342.

CESSNA MODEL 525 CITATIONJET

Dimensions: Span, 46 ft 9½ in (14,26 m); length, 42 ft 7¼ in (12,98 m); height, 13 ft 8½ in (4,18 m); wing area, 240 sq ft (22,30 m²).

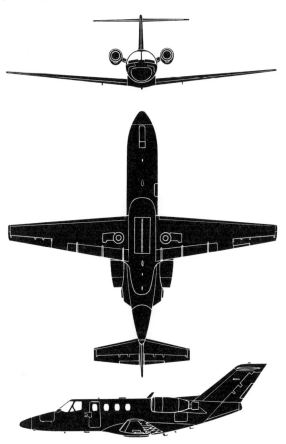

CESSNA MODEL 650/660 CITATION VI/VII

Country of Origin: USA.

Type: Light corporate executive transport.

Power Plant: Two (VI) 3,650 lb st (16,24 kN) Garrett TFE731-3B-100S or (VII) 4,000 lb st (17,79 kN) TFE731-4R-2S turbofans.

Performance: (Citation VII) Max cruise at 35,000 ft (10 670 m) and 18,000 lb (8,165 kg) cruise weight, 550 mph (885 km/h); range cruise, 500 mph (806 km/h); max initial climb, 3,700 ft/min (18,8 m/sec); certificated ceiling, 51,000 ft (15 545 m); range, (45-min reserve and allowances), 2,533 mls (4 077 km).

Weights: (Citation VII) Standard empty, 11,686 lb (5 300 kg); max take-off, 22,450 lb (10 185 kg).

Accommodation: Flight crew of two. Six passengers in individual seats in standard cabin arrangement. Up to a maximum of nine passengers.

Status: (Citation VI) First aircraft rolled out 2 January 1991, deliveries commenced March 1991. (Citation VII) Engineering prototype first flown February 1991. US certification (Citation VII) January and first delivery February 1992. Introduction of Citation VI and VII follows construction of 200 Citation IIIs.

Notes: Citation VI was announced in 1990 as a low-cost version of the Citation III (see 1991/92 Edition), with which it shares the same weights, dimensions and performance. Simplified avionics are fitted and customised interiors are not available. Citation VII is a more powerful version of the Citation III, having the same overall dimensions but different weights and performance as set out above. Launch of the Citation VI and VII followed Cessna's decision to abandon the Citation IV.

Dimensions: Span, 53 ft 6 in (16,31 m); length, 55 ft 5½ in (16,90 m); height, 16 ft 9½ in (5,12 m); wing area, 312 sq ft (29,0 m²).

CESSNA MODEL 750 CITATION X

Country of Origin: USA.

Type: Long-range corporate executive transport.

Power Plant: Two 6,000 lb st (26,69 kN) Allison GMA 3007A turbofans.

Performance: Max cruise at 37,000 ft (11 275 m) at mid-cruise weight, 580 mph (934 km/h) or Mach=0·88; range cruise, 529 mph (851 km/h); max initial climb, 4,400 ft/min (22,4 m/sec); max operating altitude, 51,000 ft (15 545 m); range, with 45-min reserve plus allowances, 3,800 mls (6 115 km).

Weights: Standard empty, 18,600 lb (8 440 kg); max take-off, 31,000 lb (14 060 kg).

Accommodation: Flight crew of two. Up to 12 passengers in cabin, with individual seats and couches.

Status: Programme announced October 1990. First flight scheduled for March 1993 with service entry expected to follow in June 1995.

Notes: Although retaining the same fuselage cross-section as the Citation III, the Model 750 Citation X ('ten') is almost wholly a new aircraft, featuring an advanced wing that allows a very high cruising speed to be achieved. According to Cessna claims, the Citation X will be the 'fastest commercial aircraft in the world apart from Concorde'. Wing sweepback is 35 deg, compared with the 25 deg of the Citation III, VI and VII. Development of the Citation X, as Cessna's 'top of the range' corporate transport, was undertaken to replace earlier plans for a less ambitious stretch of the Citation III as the Citation IV, this latter having been abandoned during 1990. Transatlantic and US transcontinental capability is planned.

Dimensions: Span, 62 ft 0 in (18,90 m); length, 64 ft 6 in (19,66 m); height, 16 ft 8½ in (5,09 m).

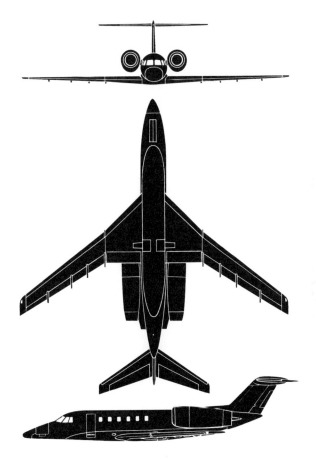

CESSNA MODEL 208 GRAND COMMANDER

Country of Origin: USA.

Type: Light commercial utility and business aircraft.

Power Plant: One 675 shp (503 kW) Pratt & Whitney Canada PT6A-114A turboprop.

Performance: Max cruise speed, 209 mph (337 km/h) at 10,000 ft (3 050 m); max initial climb, 975 ft/min (4,94 m/sec); max operating altitude, 25,000 ft (7 620 m); max range (with 45-min reserves), 1,036 mls (1 667 km) at 10,000 ft (3 050 m).

Weights: Standard empty, 4,103 lb (1 861 kg); max take-off, 8,750 lb (3 969 kg).

Accommodation: Pilot and up to nine passengers (including one alongside pilot) or 3,500 lb (1 587 kg) of freight in standard configuration.

Status: Engineering prototype of Model 208 flown on 9 December 1982 and customer deliveries began in February 1985, followed by a military version (U-27A) in 1986. The Model 208B (with lengthened fuselage) flown in prototype form on 3 March 1986, certificated in October and first delivered to Federal Express (as Super Cargomaster) on 31 October 1986. Long-fuselage Grand Commander first delivered in 1991. Total sales by early 1992, about 500.

Notes: The original Model 208 Caravan I has a fuselage length of 37 ft 7 in (11,46 m) and is windowless in its Cargomaster version developed for Federal Express. Latter company has ordered a total of 349 Cargomasters and lengthened Model 208B Super Cargomasters (illustrated above). Floatplane versions are also available.

Dimensions: Span, 52 ft 1 in (15,87 m); length, 41 ft 7 in (12,67 m); height, 14 ft 2 in (4,32 m); wing area, 279·4 sq ft (25,96 m²).

DASSAULT ATLANTIQUE 2 (ATL 2)

Country of Origin: France.

Type: Long-range maritime patrol aircraft.

Power Plant: Two 6,100 ehp (4,549 kW) Rolls-Royce Tyne RTy 20 Mk 21 turboprops.

Performance: Max speed, 402 mph (648 km/h) at optimum altitude, 368 mph (592 km/h) at sea level; max continuous cruise, 345 mph (586 km/h) at 25,000 ft (7 620 m); max initial climb (at 88,185 lb/40 000 kg), 2,000 ft/min (10,1 m/sec); patrol time (basic mission), 8 hrs at 690 mls (1 112 km) from base, (max), 11 hrs; ferry range, 5,635 mls (9 075 km).

Weights: Empty equipped, 56,320 lb (25 547 kg); max take-off (basic mission), 97,230 lb (44 103 kg); max permissible take-off, 111,640 lb (50 640 kg).

Accommodation: Normal crew of 10–12, comprising two pilots, one flight engineer, one mission tactical co-ordinator, five systems operators and two–three observers.

Armament: Up to eight Mk 46 torpedoes, nine 550-lb (250-kg) bombs, or 12 depth charges and two AM 39 Exocet ASMs. Four underwing stations for up to 7,716 lb (3 500 kg) of stores.

Status: First of two prototypes (converted ATL 1s) flown 8 May 1981, and first series ATL 2 flown 19 October 1988. First acceptance by *Aéronavale* on 26 October 1989, and six delivered by 1992 when production tempo of three annually was being maintained to meet total requirement for 42 aircraft, with completion scheduled for the year 2001.

Notes: The Atlantique 2 (ATL 2) is a modernised version of the ATL 1, production of which ended in 1973 after 87 series aircraft had been built. The Italian Navy is upgrading its ATL 1s with ATL 2 weapons systems, and a variant with auxiliary podded engines is proposed.

DASSAULT ATLANTIQUE 2 (ATL 2)

Dimensions: Span, 122 ft 9¼ in (37,42 m); length, 103 ft 9 in (31,62 m); height, 35 ft 8¾ in (10,89 m); wing area, 1,295·3 sq ft (120,34 m²).

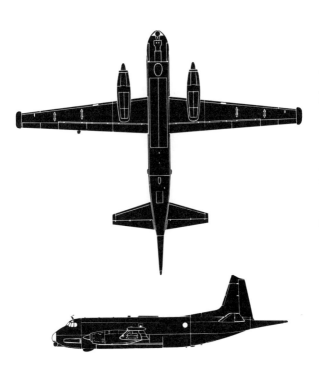

DASSAULT FALCON 900B

Country of Origin: France.

Type: Light corporate executive transport.

Power Plant: Three 4,500 lb st (20 kN) Garrett TFE731-5AR-1C or (900B) 4,750 lb st (21,13 kN) TFE731-5B turbofans.

Performance: Max speed (at 27,000 lb/12 250 kg), 574 mph (924 km/h) at 36,000 ft (10 975 m), or Mach = 0·87; max cruise, 554 mph (892 km/h) at 39,000 ft (11 890 m), or Mach = 0·84; econ cruise, 495 mph (797 km/h) at 37,000 ft (11 275 m), or Mach = 0·75; max operating altitude, 51,000 ft (15 550 m); range (max payload and IFR reserves), 3,984 mls (6 412 km), (with 15 passengers), 4,329 mls (6 968 km), (with eight passengers and 45-min reserve), 4,600 mls (7 410 km).

Weights: Operational empty (typical), 23,248 lb (10 545 kg); max take-off, 45,500 lb (20 640 kg).

Accommodation: Flight crew of two and optional main cabin arrangements for 8–15 passengers, with maximum seating for 19 passengers three abreast.

Status: Two prototypes flown on 21 September 1984 and 30 August 1985. Certification 14 March 1986, followed by first customer delivery on 19 December 1986 and 106 aircraft delivered by the beginning of 1992.

Notes: The Falcon 900 is the largest member of the Mystère-Falcon family of corporate transports and has been adopted by several countries for governmental transportation tasks. Commencing with aircraft No 107, the uprated -5B engines are used (see above), giving this Falcon 900B version improved performance including an increase of some 115 mls (185 km) in full-payload range. Earlier aircraft can be retrofitted.

DASSAULT FALCON 900

Dimensions: Span, 63 ft 5 in (19,33 m); length, 66 ft 3⅔ in (20,21 m); height, 24 ft 9¼ in (7,55 m); wing area, 527·77 sq ft (49,03 m²).

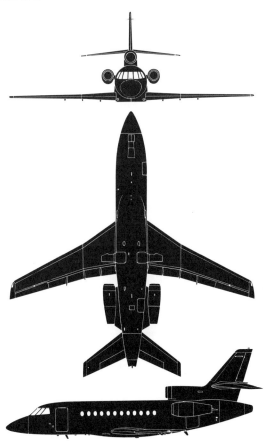

DASSAULT FALCON 2000

Country of Origin: France.

Type: Long-range corporate executive transport.

Power Plant: Two 6,000 lb st (26,7 kN) General Electric/Garrett CFE738 turbofans.

Performance: (Estimated) Max cruising speed at 39,000 ft (11 890 m), 561 mph (903 km/h) or Mach = 0·85; max certificated ceiling, 47,000 ft (14 330 m); max fuel range with eight passengers and NBAA reserves, 3,450 mls (5 550 km).

Weights: Operational empty, 19,520 lb (8 855 kg); max take-off, 35,000 lb (15 875 kg).

Accommodation: Flight crew of two. Up to 12 passengers in cabin, according to arrangement, but typically eight passenger seats. Full programme launch 4 October 1990.

Status: Preliminary details announced (as the Falcon X) in June 1989. First flight set for first quarter of 1993, with deliveries to commence end-1994 when certification completed. About 40 on option beginning of 1992.

Notes: The Falcon 2000 is a wide-body corporate transport, intended to complement the longer-range three-engined Falcon 900 and somewhat smaller Falcon 50 of similar configuration. Dassault has confirmed that it does not intend to replace the original twin-engined Falcon 20/200 and the smaller Falcon 10/100, in order to concentrate on the market for larger-capacity executive jets. The Falcon 2000 uses the wing of the Falcon 50/900, slightly modified to have the inboard slats removed and a modified leading-edge. The fuselage has the same cross-section as the Falcon 900 (see pages 86–87), but is some 6 ft 6 in (1,98 m) shorter and is redesigned to eliminate the third engine of the latter.

DASSAULT FALCON 2000

Dimensions: Span, 63 ft 5 in (19,33 m); length, 66 ft 4½ in (20,23 m); height, 22 ft 11 in (6,99 m); wing area, 527·66 sq ft (49,02 m²).

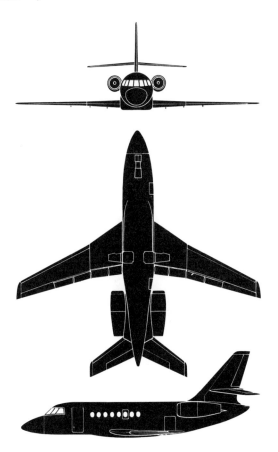

DASSAULT MIRAGE 2000-5

Country of Origin: France.
Type: Single- or two-seat multi-role fighter.
Power Plant: One 14,460 lb st (64·3 kN) dry and 21,385 lb st (95·1 kN) SNECMA M53-P2 turbofan.
Performance: Max speed (short endurance dash), 1,485 mph (2 390 km/h) above 36,090 ft (11 000 m), or Mach = 2·25, (continuous), 1,386 mph (2 230 km/h), or Mach = 2·1, (low altitude with two laser-guided ASMs or bombs, laser designation and FLIR pods, and two Magic AAMs), 695 mph (1 118 km/h), or Mach = 0·912; range (with one 286 Imp gal/1 300 l and two 374 Imp gal/1 700 l drop tanks), 2,073 mls (3 335 km); max initial climb, 60,000 ft/min (305 m/sec); time to 50,000 ft (15 240 m) and Mach = 2·0, 4·2 min.
Weights: Empty, 16,534 lb (7 500 kg); combat take-off, 20,943 lb (9 500 kg); max take-off, 33,070 lb (15 000 kg).
Armament: (Air Defence) Two 30-mm DEFA cannon, two Magic 2 short-range IR and four Mica medium-range active radar AAMs, or up to 13,890 lb (6 300 kg) of external ordnance.
Status: First (two-seat) prototype of Mirage 2000-5 flown on 24 October 1990, with second (single-seat) prototype following on 27 April 1991. No production orders for this version of the Mirage 2000 had been placed by beginning of 1992.
Notes: The Mirage 2000-5 is an enhanced multi-role development of earlier Mirage 2000 series, with RDY radar, MICA missiles and a major cockpit upgrade. At the beginning of 1992, 476 Mirage 2000s had been ordered including 157 for export (Abu Dhabi, 36, Egypt, 20, Greece, 40, India, 49 and Peru, 12).

DASSAULT MIRAGE 2000-5

Dimensions: Span, 29 ft 11½ in (9,13 m); length, 47 ft 1⅓ in (14,36 m); height, 16 ft 5⅔ in (5,02 m); wing area, 441·3 sq ft (41,00 m²).

DASSAULT RAFALE M

Country of Origin: France.
Type: Single-seat shipboard interceptor and multi-role fighter.
Power Plant: Two 10,950 lb st (48·7 kN) dry and 16,400 lb st (72·9 kN) afterburning SNECMA M88-2 turbofans.
Performance: (Estimated) Max speed, 1,320 mph (2 124 km/h) above 36,000 ft (10 975 m), or Mach = 2·0, 865 mph (1 390 km/h) at low altitude, or Mach = 1·15; tactical radius (air-to-air mission with eight Mica AAMs, one 374 Imp gal/1 700 l centreline tank and two 286 Imp gal/1 300 l underwing tanks), 1,152 mls (1 853 km), (HI-LO-LO-HI penetration with 12 551-lb/250-kg bombs, four Mica AAMs and 946 Imp gal/4 300 l external fuel), 679 mls (1 093 km).
Weights: (Estimated) Empty equipped, 21,605 lb (9 800 kg); max take-off, 42,990 lb (19 500 kg).
Armament: One 30-mm GiAT DEFA 791 cannon and normal maximum external ordnance load (distributed between 13 stations) of 13,228 lb (6 000 kg), with maximum permissible load of 17,637 lb (8 000 kg).
Status: First of four prototypes (Rafale C) flown on 19 May 1991, with second prototype (the first navalised Rafale M) following on 12 December 1991. The third prototype (Rafale B) expected to fly February 1993, with final prototype (second Rafale M) following mid 1995. Current planning calls for production of 80 Rafale Ms for the *Aéronavale* and up to 250 Rafale Bs for the *Armée de l'Air*, with deliveries commencing 1997.
Notes: During 1991, the single-seat Rafale C was overtaken by the tandem two-seat Rafale B in *Armée de l'Air* procurement planning, but the former will be available for export. The Rafale M is, together with the Rafale B, a production derivative of the Rafale A advanced fighter technology demonstrator.

DASSAULT RAFALE M

Dimensions: Span (over wingtip missiles), 35 ft $9\frac{1}{8}$ in (10,90 m); length, 50 ft $2\frac{1}{3}$ in (15,30 m); wing area, 484·39 sq ft (45,00 m²).

DE HAVILLAND DASH 8-300A

Country of Origin: Canada.

Type: Regional commercial transport.

Power Plant: Two 2,380 shp (1 775 kW) Pratt & Whitney Canada PW123 or (option) 2,500 shp (1 864 kW) turboprops.

Performance: Max cruise speed (at 40,850 lb/18 530 kg), 330 mph (531 km/h) at 15,000 ft (4 575 m); max initial climb, 1,800 ft/min (9,1 m/sec); certificated ceiling, 25,000 ft (7 620 m); range (50 passengers with IFR reserves), 967 mls (1 556 km), (optional long-range version), 1,440 mls (2 315 km).

Weights: Operational empty, 25,700 lb (11 657 kg); max take-off, 41,100 lb (18 643 kg), optional, 43,000 lb (19 505 kg).

Accommodation: Flight crew of two and up to 56 passengers, four abreast with single aisle. Standard arrangement for 50 passengers.

Status: Dash 8-300 prototype (converted from Dash 8-100) flown on 15 May 1987, with first customer delivery (to Time Air) following on 27 February 1989. First Srs 300A high gross weight option delivery (to Contact Air) on 24 August 1990 and first with PW123B engine option (to Tyrolean Airways) in 1991. Orders (all versions) totalled 379 (263 Srs 100, 116 Srs 300) as of 1 February 1992, with 300 delivered.

Notes: The Dash 8-300 series is a stretched version of the original -100 series with fore and aft fuselage plugs totalling 11 ft 3 in (3,43 m), increased wing span, strengthened undercarriage and more powerful engines. Basic aircraft is Srs 301; the Srs 320B (and Srs 320C Combi) introduced higher gross weight as indicated above and is marketed as the Dash 8-300A. Srs 200 is a Srs 100 with derated PW123s and other Srs 300 features, to be available summer 1993. De Havilland was a division of Boeing Canada from 1986, and was acquired in 1992 by Bombardier in association with the Province of Ontario.

DE HAVILLAND DASH 8-300A

Dimensions: Span, 90 ft 0 in (27,43 m); length, 84 ft 3 in (25,68 m); height, 24 ft 7 in (7,49 m); wing area, 605 sq ft (56,21 m²).

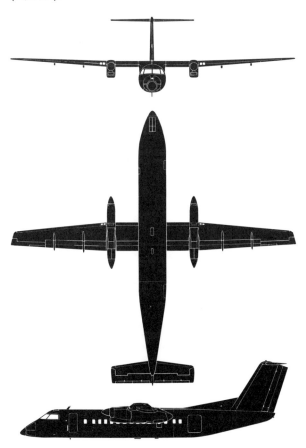

DORNIER (DASA) 328

Country of Origin: Germany.

Type: Light regional commercial transport.

Power Plant: Two 2,300 shp (1 735 kW) Pratt & Whitney Canada PW119A turboprops.

Performance: (Estimated) Max cruise speed, 398 mph (640 km/h) at 25,000 ft (7 620 m); max initial climb, 2,430 ft/min (12,34 m/sec); cruising ceiling, 31,000 ft (9 450 m); range (30 passengers and allowances for 115-ml/185-km diversion and 45-min hold), 808 mls (1 300 km), (16 passengers), 1,727 mls (2 780 km).

Weights: Operational empty, 18,022 lb (8 175 kg); max take-off, 27,557 lb (12 500 kg).

Accommodation: Flight crew of two and 30–33 passengers three abreast with maximum seating for 39 passengers four abreast.

Status: First flight of first of two prototypes, 6 December 1991, with second scheduled for April 1992 and European JAR certification, followed by FAA approval, set for early 1993. First delivery (to Sunshine Aviation) April 1993 and first to USA (Horizon Air) June 1993. Orders totalled 45 plus 30 options at the beginning of 1992.

Notes: The Dornier 328, developed by the Dornier Luftfahrt subsidiary of Deutsche Aerospace, retains the basic wing profile of the smaller Dornier 228, with an enlarged centre section and new flap system, combining this with a new, larger circular-section fuselage. Offering short take-off and landing characteristics, the 328 can operate from rough, unprepared strips. Current planning includes a stretched version, the Dornier 328S with 48/50-seat capacity, a corporate executive transport version (for which the first order had been placed by the beginning of 1991), civil and military freighters, and a surveillance version.

DORNIER (DASA) 328

Dimensions: Span, 68 ft 10 in (20,98 m); Length, 69 ft 10 in (21,28 m); height, 23 ft 7½ in (7,20 m).

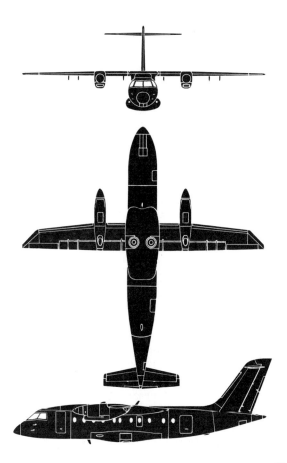

EMBRAER EMB-120 BRASILIA

Country of Origin: Brazil.

Type: Short-haul regional transport.

Power Plant: Two 1,800 shp (1 342 kW) Pratt & Whitney Canada PW118 or PW118A turboprops.

Performance: (PW118A engines) Max speed, 378 mph (608 km/h) at 20,000 ft (6 100 m); max cruise, 357 mph (574 km/h) at 25,000 ft (7 620 m); max initial climb, 2,120 ft/min (10,77 m/sec); service ceiling, 32,000 ft (9 755 m); range (with 30 passengers), 576 mls (925 km).

Weights: Operational empty, 16,457 lb (7 465 kg); max take-off, 25,353 lb (11 500 kg).

Accommodation: Flight crew of two and standard arrangements for 30 passengers in three-abreast seating. Also available are a mixed-traffic version for 24 or 26 passengers, an all-cargo version and an executive transport version.

Status: First of three prototypes was flown on 27 July 1983, with first customer delivery (to Atlantic Southeast Airlines) in June 1985. 200th Brasilia delivered in August 1990. 'Hot and high' version (PW118A engines) first delivered in 1986. First corporate Brasilia delivered (to UTC) in September 1986. Production rate at 3·5 a month in 1991; orders for 308 by early 1992, of which 242 had been delivered.

Notes: Apart from corporate and regional transport versions, the Brasilia is offered for a variety of military roles and is used with the VC-97 designation by the Brazilian Air Force as a VIP transport. An extended-range version (EMB-120ER) became available in 1991, for new deliveries or as a retrofit. This has a gross weight of 26,455 lb (12 000 kg) and a full-passenger payload range of 1,035 mls (1 666 km).

Dimensions: Span, 64 ft 10¾ in (19,78 m); length, 65 ft 7½ in (20,00 m); height, 20 ft 10 in (6,35 m); wing area, 424·42 sq ft (39,43 m²).

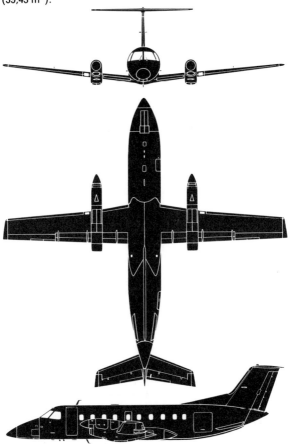

EMBRAER EMB-312H TUCANO H

Country of Origin: Brazil.

Type: Tandem two-seat basic/advanced trainer.

Power Plant: One 1,600 shp (1 190 kW) Pratt & Whitney Canada PT6A-67R turboprop.

Performance: No details available at the time of closing for press.

Weights: Max take-off (clean), 6,107 lb (2 770 kg), (with external stores), 7,518 lb (3 410 kg).

Armament: (Light strike and weapons training) Provision for two hardpoints under each wing each stressed for a maximum load of 551 lb (250 kg).

Status: The proof-of-concept EMB-312H was first flown on 9 September 1991. No production plans for this trainer had been announced early 1992 when manufacture of the basic EMB-312 was being resumed.

Notes: The EMB-312H Tucano H is a progressive development of the EMB-312 (see 1991/92 edition). The 750 shp (559 kW) PT6A-25C engine and four-bladed propeller of the latter are replaced by a PT6A-67R engine affording twice as much power and a five-bladed propeller; zero-zero ejection seats are introduced, together with pressure refuelling and an on-board oxygen generating system, and CG range is maintained by the insertion of additional sections fore and aft of the cockpit. The EMB-312H will, it is claimed, attain speeds normally associated with pure jet aircraft and will be capable of undertaking half the advanced training syllabus of a pure jet trainer. Total orders and options for the standard EMB-312 were claimed to be 641 aircraft for 12 air forces at the beginning of 1992 (including the Shorts-built S312) of which 476 had been delivered. In October 1991, an order was signed on behalf of France's *Armée de l'Air* for two Tucanos (embodying strengthened wings similar to those of the S312) with options on a further 25 aircraft.

EMBRAER EMB-312H TUCANO H

Dimensions: Span, 36 ft 6½ in (11,14 m); length, 37 ft 5⅔ in (11,42 m); height, 12 ft 0¾ in (3,68 m); wing area, 208·82 sq ft (19,40 m²).

EMBRAER/FMA CBA-123 VECTOR

Countries of Origin: Brazil and Argentina.

Type: Light regional airliner and corporate transport.

Power Plant: Two 1,300 shp (969 kW) Garrett TPF351-20 or -20A turboprops.

Performance (Manufacturer's estimates): Max cruise speed, 404 mph (650 km/h) at 24,000 ft (7 315 m); max initial climb, 2,350 ft/min (11,94 m/sec); service ceiling, 36,000 ft (11 000 m); range (19 passengers and IFR reserves), 978 mls (1 575 km), range (max fuel), 2,140 mls (3 447 km).

Weights: Operational empty, 13,816 lb (6 267 kg); max take-off, 20,944 lb (9 500 kg).

Accommodation: Flight crew of two and standard commuter arrangement for 19 passengers (plus flight attendant) three abreast with four seats on rear cabin bulkhead.

Status: First of five prototypes (including structural and fatigue test specimens) flown (in Brazil) on 18 July 1990 with second (also in Brazil) flown on 15 March 1991 and third (in Argentina) later in 1991. Certification anticipated in March 1992 but production launch dependent on firm orders being obtained for a minimum of 20 aircraft.

Notes: The Vector was developed jointly by Embraer (80 per cent) in Brazil and FMA (20 per cent) in Argentina, each company planning final assembly lines without component manufacturing duplication. Innovative in having its turboprops pylon-mounted on the rear fuselage and driving six-bladed pusher propellers, the Vector utilises a shortened version of the EMB-120 Brasilia fuselage. Its manufacturers hoped to gain 30 per cent of the calculated 2,000-aircraft market for 19-seaters between 1992 and 2005 but prospects for a production launch became uncertain after the early nineties downturn in the commuter market.

EMBRAER/FMA CBA-123 VECTOR

Dimensions: Span, 58 ft 1 in (17,72 m); length, 59 ft 4¼ in (18,09 m); height, 19 ft 7 in (5,97 m); wing area, 292·79 sq ft (27,20 m²).

EUROFIGHTER EFA

Countries of Origin: United Kingdom, Germany, Italy and Spain.

Type: Single-seat air defence and air superiority fighter.

Power Plant: Two approx 13,490 lb st (60 kN) dry and 20,250 lb st (90 kN) afterburning Eurojet EJ200 turbofans.

Performance: (Estimated) Max speed, 1,190–1,255 mph (1 915–2 020 km/h) above 36,000 ft (10 975 m), or Mach = 1·8 to 1·9; combat radius (two AIM-120 and two AIM-132 AAMs), 350 mls (565 km).

Weights: (Estimated) Empty, 21,495 lb (9 750 kg); max take-off, 46,297 lb (21 000 kg).

Armament: One 27-mm Mauser cannon and mix of four medium-range AIM-120 AAMs and up to six short-range AIM-9 or AIM-132 AAMs.

Status: First of seven prototypes scheduled to enter flight test (in Germany) in September 1992, with second following (in UK) shortly afterwards. All prototypes are expected to have entered flight test by 1994, with first production aircraft flying in 1996–97. Approximately 600–650 aircraft planned by partner nations.

Notes: The EFA (European Fighter Aircraft) is being developed in both single- and two-seat versions by an international consortium of the UK and Germany (each responsible for 33 per cent), Italy (21 per cent) and Spain (13 per cent). The first two prototypes are powered by the Turbo-Union RB199-122 turbofan, and the third and seventh are to be two-seaters. The fifth and sixth prototypes will be the main avionics test beds.

EUROFIGHTER EFA

Dimensions: Span, 34 ft 5½ in (10,50 m); length, 47 ft 7 in (14,50 m); wing area, 538·2 sq ft (50,00 m²).

FAIRCHILD METRO 23

Country of Origin: USA.

Type: Light regional commercial transport.

Power Plant: Two 1,100 shp (820 kW) Garrett TPE331-12UAR turboprops.

Performance: Cruising speed at mid-cruise weight, 335 mph (539 km/h) at 13,000 ft (3 962 m); max initial climb, 2,730 ft/min (13,8 m/sec); range with 19 passengers, 1,180 mls (1 900 km).

Weights: Operational empty, 9,377 lb (4 253 kg); max take-off, 16,500 lb (7 483 kg).

Accommodation: Flight crew of two. Standard arrangement for 19 passengers two-abreast with central aisle.

Status: Metro (SA227) prototype first flown 26 August 1969, certificated 11 June 1970. Customer deliveries (to Air Wisconsin) began 1973. Metro II introduced 1974. Metro IIA certificated to SFAR-41 on 23 June 1980. Metro III entered service 1981. Metro IIIA first flown 31 December 1981 (with Pratt & Whitney PT6A-45R turboprops). Metro III-11 certificated June 1990 and Metro 23 certificated September 1990 to FAR 23 requirements for commuter aircraft.

Notes: Metro 23 is latest of the Metro family of commuter aircraft, its designation indicating certification to the latest FAR 23 standard. Compared with Metro III (production of which ended late 1991), the Metro 23 has higher-rated engines, higher weights and various systems and performance improvements developed for the C-26A and C-26B military variants used by US ANG. Metro 23 (EF) features an 'expanded fuselage' comprising a deepening of the bottom line (see silhouette) over a length of 32 ft (9,75 m) to provide an extra 115 cu ft (3,26 m³) of baggage capacity. The name Expediter is used for all-cargo version of Metro III/23 and corporate transport equivalents are known as Merlin IVs.

Dimensions: Span, 57 ft 0 in (17,37 m); length, 59 ft $4\frac{1}{4}$ in (18,09 m); height, 16 ft 8 in (5,08 m); wing area, 309 sq ft (28,71 m²).

FFT EUROTRAINER 2000A

Country of Origin: Germany.

Type: Side-by-side two-seat primary/basic trainer and two-plus-two-seat touring aircraft.

Power Plant: One 270 hp (201 kW) Textron Lycoming AEIO-540-L1B5 six-cylinder horizontally-opposed engine.

Performance: (Manufacturer's estimates) Max cruise speed, 212 mph (341 km/h) at sea level, 204 mph (328 km/h) at 8,000 ft (2 438 m); initial climb rate, 1,338 ft/min (6,80 m/sec); service ceiling, 20,000 ft (6 100 m); max range, 1,122 mls (1 806 km).

Weights: Empty, 2,028 lb (920 kg); max take-off (aerobatic), 2,866 lb (1 300 kg), (utility), 3,263 lb (1 480 kg).

Accommodation: Seats for two or four persons in pairs under one-piece hinged canopy.

Status: The prototype Eurotrainer 2000A made its first flight on 8 June 1991, and the first of eight aircraft ordered for Swissair's civil aviation flying school was expected to be delivered following certification in March 1992.

Notes: The Eurotrainer 2000A, which is built entirely of composite materials, was originally developed by the FFA Flugzeugwerke Altenrhein AG (formerly Flug- und Fahrzeugwerke AG), which transferred all its aviation activities at the end of 1989 to the Gesellschaft für Flugzeug- und Faserverbund Technologie (FFT), (formerly Gyroflug GmbH) of Mengen, Germany – itself a member of the Zurich-based Justus Dornier Group. The Eurotrainer is intended for *ab initio* tuition, screening, navigational instruction and basic aerobatic training, and is stressed for +6*g* and −3*g*. The design makes provision for the introduction of an additional pair of seats when the aircraft is used as a tourer.

Dimensions: Span, 34 ft 0¾ in (10,38 m); length, 26 ft 8½ in (8,14 m); height, 10 ft 6 in (3,20 m); wing area, 150·7 sq ft (14,00 m²).

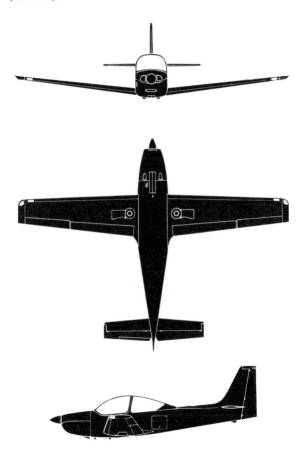

FMA IA 63 PAMPA

Country of Origin: Argentina.

Type: Tandem two-seat basic/advanced trainer.

Power Plant: One (first 18 aircraft) 3,500 lb st (15·57 kN) Garrett TFE731-2-2N or (subsequent) 4,500 lb st (20·02 kN) TFE731-3G turbofan.

Performance: (TFE731-2-2N) Max speed, 509 mph (819 km/h) at 22,965 ft (7 000 m), 466 mph (750 km/h) at sea level; max cruise, 464 mph (747 km/h) at 13,125 ft (4 000 m); max initial climb, 5,950 ft/min (30,23 m/sec); service ceiling, 42,325 ft (12 900 m); range (max internal fuel), 932 mls (1 500 km) at 345 mph (556 km/h) at 13,125 ft (4 000 m).

Weights: Empty, 6,219 lb (2 821 kg); loaded (aerobatic) 8,377 lb (3 800 kg); max take-off, 11,023 lb (5 000 kg).

Armament: (Armament training or light attack) One 30-mm cannon pod on fuselage centreline. Max ordnance load (including cannon) of 2,557 lb (1 160 kg) distributed between centreline and four wing stations.

Status: First of three prototypes flown on 6 October 1984, and first three series aircraft delivered to Argentine Air Force on 15 March 1988. Total requirement of Argentine Air Force for 65 aircraft.

Notes: The Pampa was developed on behalf of the Argentine government by the German Dornier concern and is being manufactured in series by the FMA (Fabrica Militar de Aviones). The more powerful TFE731-3G engine has been standardised from the nineteenth aircraft, and two of the prototypes have been evaluated with more advanced avionics and a head-up display. The FMA has linked with the LTV Corporation to submit a 'missioned' version of the Pampa as a contender in the JPATS (USAF and USN Joint Primary Aircraft Training System) contest as the Pampa 2000.

Dimensions: Span, 31 ft 9½ in (9,69 m); length, 35 ft 9¼ in (10,90 m); height, 14 ft 0¾ in (4,29 m); wing area, 168·24 sq ft (15,63 m²).

FOKKER 50

Country of Origin: Netherlands.
Type: Regional commercial transport.
Power Plant: Two 2,500 shp (1,864 kW) Pratt & Whitney Canada PW125B turboprops.
Performance: Max cruise speed, 330 mph (532 km/h) at 20,000 ft (6 100 m); range cruise, 282 mph (454 km/h); max operating altitude, 25,000 ft (7 620 m); range (with 50 passengers and 45 min reserves), 1,277 mls (2 055 km), (at optional high gross weight), 1,754 mls (2 822 km).
Weights: Operational empty (typical), 27,602 lb (12 520 kg); max take-off (standard), 43,982 lb (19 950 kg), (optional), 45,900 lb (20 820 kg).
Accommodation: Flight crew of two and standard arrangement for 50 passengers four abreast, with optional high-density seating for 58 passengers.
Status: First of two prototypes (based on F27 airframes) flown on 28 December 1985, with first customer delivery (to DLT) following on 7 August 1987. Firm orders and options for 155 aircraft by beginning of 1992, plus 14 options, with production rate scheduled to be 33 aircraft per year from 1991 onwards. First order for Enforcer Mk 2 placed by Singapore in 1991.
Notes: Based on the F27-500 Friendship airframe, the Fokker 50 Srs 100 embodies significant design and structural changes. The 2,750 shp (2 050 kW) PW127A engine has been adopted for the Srs 300 'hot and high' version of the Fokker 50 launched in 1990. The Srs 400 is a proposed 'stretch' for up to 68 passengers, with 2,750 shp (2 050 kW) PW127Bs. Srs 120, 320 and 420 designations apply to a three-door configuration, with large cargo door in rear fuselage in place of a smaller door each side. Enforcer Mk 2 is paramilitary version for maritime patrol.

Dimensions: Span, 95 ft 1¾ in (29,00 m); length, 82 ft 10 in (25,25 m); height, 27 ft 3½ in (8,32 m); wing area, 753·5 sq ft (70,00 m²).

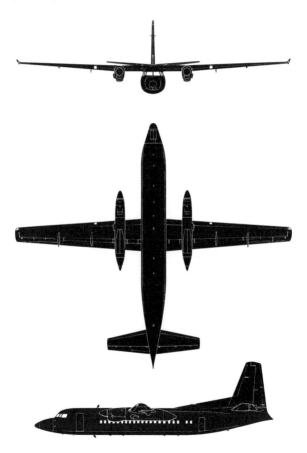

FOKKER 100

Country of Origin: Netherlands.

Type: Short- to medium-haul commercial transport.

Power Plant: Two 13,850 lb st (61·6 kN) Rolls-Royce Tay 620-15 or 15,100 lb st (67·2 kN) Tay 650-15 turbofans.

Performance: Max cruise speed, 525 mph (845 km/h) at 27,000 ft (8 230 m); range cruise, 458 mph (737 km/h) at 35,000 ft (10 670 m); service ceiling, 35,000 ft (10 670 m); range (Tay 620 with 107 passengers), 1,554 mls (2 502 km), (Tay 650, high gross weight), 1,969 mls (3 167 km).

Weights: Operational empty (Tay 620), 53,738 lb (24 375 kg), (Tay 650), 54,103 lb (24 541 kg); max take-off (Tay 620), 95,000 lb (43 090 kg), (Tay 650), 98,000–101,000 lb (44 450–45 810 kg).

Accommodation: Flight crew of two and standard arrangement for 107 passengers five abreast. Optional layouts include 12 first-class and 85 economy-class four and five abreast respectively, or 55 business- and 50 economy-class, all five abreast. Maximum, 122 passengers.

Status: First of two prototypes flown 30 November 1986, with first customer delivery (to Swissair) following on 25 February 1987. Total of 242 on firm order (plus 115 on option) at the beginning of 1992, with more than 70 delivered and production rising to 67 annually by 1993.

Notes: A derivative of the F28 Fellowship, the Fokker 100 makes extensive use of advanced technology, has new systems and equipment, new engines, a lengthened fuselage and revised wing aerodynamics. As part of its JetLine family, Fokker plans to launch the Fokker 70 for 1994 delivery and the Fokker 130 for 1996/97, respectively with shorter and longer fuselages. With a length of 99 ft 4 in (30,3 m), the Fokker 70 will seat 70 passengers and have a weight of 81,000 lb (36 740 kg).

Dimensions: Span, 92 ft 1½ in (28,08 m); length, 116 ft 6¾ in (35,53 m); height, 27 ft 10½ in (8,50 m); wing area, 1,006·4 sq ft (93,50 m²).

GENERAL DYNAMICS F-16 FIGHTING FALCON

Country of Origin: USA.
Type: Single-seat multi-role fighter.
Power Plant: One 23,770 lb st (105·7 kN) with afterburning Pratt & Whitney F100-PW-220 or 28,984 lb st (128·9 kN) General Electric F110-GE-100 turbofan.
Performance: (At 27,245 lb/12 356 kg with F100 engine) Max speed (short endurance dash), 1,333 mph (2 145 km/h) at 40,000 ft (12 190 m), or Mach=2·02, (sustained), 1,247 mph (2 007 km/h), or Mach=1·89; tactical radius (HI-LO-HI interdiction on internal fuel with six 500-lb/227-kg bombs), 360 mls (580 km); ferry range (max external fuel), 2,450 mls (3 943 km).
Weights: Empty, 18,238 lb (8 273 kg); normal loaded (air-to-air mission), 26,463 lb (12 000 kg); max take-off (with max external load), 42,300 lb (19 187 kg).
Armament: One 20-mm rotary cannon and up to 12,430 lb (5 638 kg) of ordnance/fuel distributed between one fuselage centreline and six underwing stations, plus wingtip stations.
Status: First of two (YF-16) prototypes flown 20 January 1974, and 3,650 production aircraft (all versions) ordered by beginning of 1992 when approximately 2,950 delivered by the parent company and from assembly lines in Belgium, Netherlands and Turkey. Assembly also to be undertaken in South Korea.
Notes: Current production models of the Fighting Falcon are the single-seat F-16C and two-seat F-16D, with those delivered from late 1991 (Block 50/52) embodying various upgrades, including increased performance Pratt & Whitney F100-PW-229 or General Electric F110-GE-129 engines and more advanced radar. Proposals have been made to modify 250 F-16Cs and Ds as attack-optimised aircraft (unofficially F/A-16s) to supplant the Fairchild A-10 in the close air support role in USAF service. Two hundred and seventy earlier F-16As and Bs as air defence fighters with AIM-7 Sparrow AAMs for the Air National Guard.

GENERAL DYNAMICS F-16 FIGHTING FALCON

Dimensions: Span (over missile launchers), 31 ft 0 in (9,45 m); length, 49 ft 4 in (15,03 m); height, 16 ft 8½ in (5,09 m); wing area, 300 sq ft (27,87 m²).

GRUMMAN E-2C HAWKEYE

Country of Origin: USA.
Type: Shipboard or shore-based airborne early warning, surface surveillance and strike control aircraft.
Power Plant: Two 5,250 shp (3,915 kW) Allison T56-A-427 turboprops.
Performance: (At 51,933 lb/23 556 kg) Max speed, 372 mph (598 km/h); max cruise, 358 mph (576 km/h); max initial climb, 2,515 ft/min (12,8 m/sec); service ceiling, 30,800 ft (9 390 m); time on station (200 mls/320 km from base), 3–4 hrs; ferry range, 1,604 mls (2 580 km).
Weights: Max take-off, 54,000 lb (24 494 kg).
Accommodation: Normal crew of five comprising pilot, co-pilot, combat information centre officer, air control officer and radar operator.
Status: First of two E-2C prototypes flown 20 January 1971, with first production aircraft (Group 1 standard) following on 23 September 1972. Total of 144 for US Navy with deliveries to be completed in 1996, and first of upgraded (Group 2 standard) model delivered to the service early 1992 with production continuing at six annually. Four supplied to Israel, total of 11 ordered by Japan, six for Egypt and four for Singapore. Four transferred by US Navy to US Coast Guard.
Notes: Evolved from the E-2A (56 of which were built with 52 upgraded to E-2B standard), the E-2C supplanted the 'blue water' capable radar of the preceding versions with radar capable of target detection and tracking over land. New-build aircraft with deliveries commencing 1992 are of Group 2 standard with -427 turboprops, increased IFF range and APS-145 radar with extended detection range and improved overland clutter resistance. Fifty-four Group 1 E-2Cs are to be retrofitted to Group 2 standards through the late 'nineties.

GRUMMAN E-2C HAWKEYE

Dimensions: Span, 80 ft 7 in (24,56 m); length, 57 ft 7 in (17,55 m); height, 18 ft 4 in (5,69 m); wing area, 700 sq ft (65,03 m²).

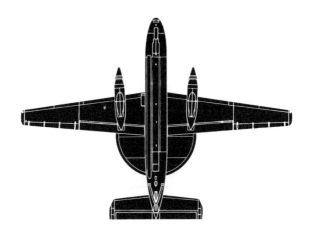

GRUMMAN F-14D SUPER TOMCAT

Country of Origin: USA.

Type: Two-seat multi-role shipboard fighter.

Power Plant: Two 14,000 lb st (62·3 kN) dry and 23,100 lb st (102·75 kN) afterburning General Electric F110-GE-400 turbofans.

Performance: Max speed (with four semi-recessed AIM-7 AAMs), 1,544 mph (2 485 km/h) at 40,000 ft (12 190 m), or Mach = 2·34, 912 mph (1 486 km/h) at sea level, or Mach = 1·2; intercept radius (at Mach = 1·3), 510 mls (820 km); combat air patrol loiter time (with external fuel), 2·7 hrs.

Weights: (Estimated) Empty, 42,000 lb (19 050 kg); max take-off, 75,000 lb (34 020 kg).

Armament: One 20-mm rotary cannon and (typical) four AIM-54C Phoenix (beneath fuselage) or AIM-7 Sparrow (semi-recessed) AAMs, plus four AIM-9 Sidewinder short-range AAMs or two additional Phoenix or Sparrow missiles on fixed-glove pylons.

Status: First new-build F-14D flown March 1990, with further 36 ordered and deliveries completed mid-1992. Remanufacturing programme to bring F-14A to similar standards as F-14D(R) initiated June 1990, with 18 aircraft (12 at Grumman and six at Naval Aircraft Depot) having entered programme by beginning of 1992 when no further contracts had been placed.

Notes: The F-14D represents the second stage in a two-stage upgrade of the F-14A of which 557 were delivered to the US Navy. The first was the F-14B, formerly F-14A(Plus), which retained similar systems to those of the F-14A, but was re-engined with the F110. The first prototype F-14B flew on 29 September 1986, with the first of 38 new-build examples following on 14 November 1987, and last being completed May 1990, 32 F-14As being converted to the same standard. The F-14D has 60 per cent new avionics, including APG-71 radar, ASN-139 digital navigation and JTIDS secure datalink.

GRUMMAN F-14D SUPER TOMCAT

Dimensions: Span (20 deg sweep), 64 ft 1½ in (19,55 m), (68 deg sweep), 38 ft 2½ in (11,65 m); length, 62 ft 8 in (19,10 m); height, 16 ft 0 in (4,88 m); wing area, 565 sq ft (52,49 m²).

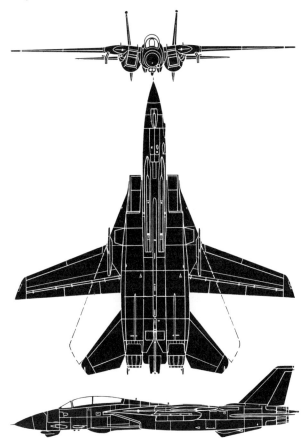

GULFSTREAM AEROSPACE GULFSTREAM IV

Country of Origin: USA.

Type: Long-range corporate executive transport.

Power Plant: Two 13,850 lb st (61·6 kN) Rolls-Royce Tay Mk 611-8 turbofans.

Performance: Max cruise speed, 586 mph (943 km/h) at 31,000 ft (9 450 m); normal cruise, 528 mph (850 km/h) at 45,000 ft (13 715 m); max initial climb, 4,000 ft/min (20,32 m/sec); max operating altitude, 45,000 ft (13 715 m); range (eight passengers, IFR reserves), 4,750 mls (7 650 km).

Weights: Empty, 42,600 lb (19 323 kg); max take-off, 74,600 lb (33 839 kg).

Accommodation: Flight crew of two or three and standard seating for 14 to 19 passengers.

Status: First of four production prototypes flown on 19 September 1985, with FAA certification being granted on 22 April 1987. More than 175 Gulfstream IVs in service by the beginning of 1992, including C-20s used by US military services.

Notes: The Gulfstream IV is an advanced version of the Gulfstream III, differing primarily in having a structurally redesigned wing incorporating 30 per cent fewer parts, more internal fuel capacity, a lengthened fuselage, a longer-span tailplane and uprated engines. Further improvements planned for introduction in 1994 include higher weights, as shown above, to give a major improvement in payload-range. A Gulfstream V is planned for introduction in the mid 'nineties, with slightly lengthened fuselage, higher weights and more range. Gulfstream IVs are used by the USAF, USN and USMC under the C-20 designation and the SRA-4 is a special missions prototype based on the Gulfstream IV airframe (see 1989/90 edition).

Dimensions: Span, 77 ft 10 in (23,72 m); length, 88 ft 4 in (26,92 m); height, 24 ft 10 in (7,57 m); wing area, 950·39 sq ft (88,29 m²).

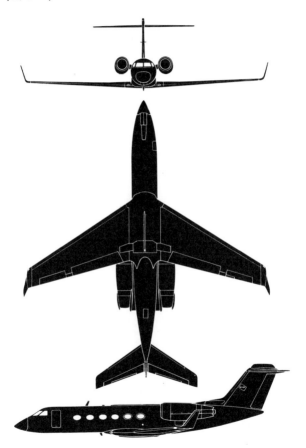

ILYUSHIN IL-96-300

Country of Origin: Commonwealth of Independent States (Russia).

Type: Long-haul commercial transport.

Power Plant: Four 35,275 lb st (156·9 kN) Perm (Soloviev) PS-90A turbofans.

Performance: (Manufacturer's estimates) Max cruise speed, 559 mph (900 km/h) at 39,700 ft (12 100 m); econ cruise, 528 mph (850 km/h) at 33,135 ft (10 100 m); range (with reserves and max payload), 4,660 mls (7 500 km) (with reserves and 33,070-lb/15 000-kg payload), 6,835 mls (11 000 km).

Weights: Basic operational, 257,936 lb (117 000 kg); max take-off, 476,200 lb (216 000 kg).

Accommodation: Flight crew of two pilots and a flight engineer plus provision for a navigator. Basic all-economy class arrangement for 300 passengers nine-abreast in two cabins. Various optional arrangements including a 235-seat mixed-class version with 22 first-class passengers six abreast, 40 business-class passengers eight abreast and 173 economy-class passengers basically nine abreast.

Status: The first of three flying prototypes was flown on 28 September 1988, the second following on 28 November 1989 and the third in 1990. Initial customer deliveries (to Aeroflot) expected in 1992. Original planning called for 60–70 Il-96s most if not all of which are now expected to be in Il-96M configuration.

Notes: Possessing a superficial resemblance to the earlier Il-86, the Il-96 is fundamentally a new design. A stretched version, the Il-96M (initially called Il-96-350) will accommodate 350 passengers and conversion of the first Il-96-300 to serve as a prototype began in 1992. Powered by 37,565 lb st (161.7 kN) Pratt & Whitney PW2037 turbofans, the Il-96M is expected to make its first flight in mid-1994, with four more, and certification, completed in 1995.

Dimensions: Span (over winglets), 197 ft 2½ in (60,11 m); length, 181 ft 7¼ in (55,35 m); height, 57 ft 7¾ in (17,57 m); wing area, 4,215 sq ft (391·6 m²).

ILYUSHIN IL-114

Country of Origin: Commonwealth of Independent States (Russia).

Type: Regional commercial transport.

Power Plant: Two 2,500 shp (1 685 kW) Leningrad KB (Isotov) TV7-117 turboprops.

Performance: (Estimated) Max cruise speed, 310 mph (500 km/h) at 26,740 ft (8 150 m); optimum cruise altitude, 19,685–26,250 ft (6 000–8 000 m); range with reserves (with 11,905 lb/5 400-kg payload), 621 mls (1 000 km), (with 7,935-lb/3 600-kg payload), 1,770 mls (2 850 km), (with 3,300-lb/1 500-kg payload), 2,980 mls (4 800 km).

Weights: Operational empty, 30,200 lb (13 700 kg); max take-off, 46,300 lb (21 000 kg).

Accommodation: Flight crew of two and basic arrangement for 60 passengers seated four abreast with central aisle.

Status: First prototype flown on 29 March 1990, with two more prototypes and two static test specimens following in programme to obtain certification in 1993. Production deliveries scheduled to begin in 1993 from assembly plant in Tashkent (Uzbekistan) with some components being contributed by Poland, Romania and Bulgaria. The Il-114 is expected to be manufactured in large numbers, production of some 500 being envisaged during the original Soviet 1990–95 five-year plan.

Notes: Intended as a successor to the Antonov An-24 in Aeroflot service, the Il-114 bears an obvious resemblance to the British Aerospace ATP. Intended to operate over Aeroflot internal routes of up to 620 miles (1 000 km) in length, the Il-114 makes extensive use of composite materials and advanced metal alloys, including titanium, in its structure, and is designed to operate from both paved and grass surfaces.

ILYUSHIN IL-114

Dimensions: Span, 98 ft 5¼ in (30,00 m); length, 86 ft 3⅔ in (26,31 m); height, 30 ft 7 in (9,32 m).

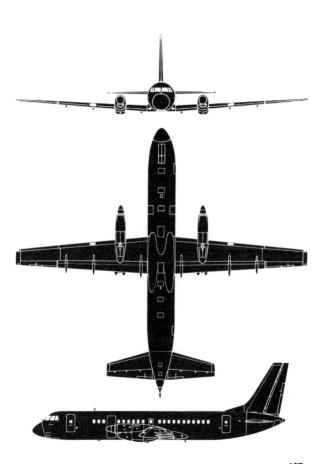

ILYUSHIN A-50 (MAINSTAY)

Country of Origin: Commonwealth of Independent States (Russia).

Type: Airborne warning and control system aircraft.

Power Plant: Four 26,455 lb st (117.7 kN) MKB (Soloviev) D-30KP turbofans.

Performance: (Estimated) Max continuous cruise speed, 475 mph (764 km/h) at 29,500–42,650 ft (9 000–13 000 m); typical loiter speed, 395 mph (636 km/h) at 29,500 ft (9 000 m); time on station (unrefuelled) at 930 mls (1 500 km) from base, 8–9 hrs.

Weights: (Estimated) Max take-off, 380,000 lb (172 370 kg).

Accommodation: Flight crew of four, plus tactical and air direction teams totalling 9–12 personnel.

Status: A derivative of the Il-76TD heavy duty transport (see 1991/92 edition), the A-50 was flown in pre-prototype form (i.e. with dorsal radome but without avionics) in 1979, with first of three fully-equipped prototypes flying late 1982. Initial operational capability was attained in 1986, and 25 reportedly in service at beginning of 1992, when production was continuing at Tashkent at a rate of four-five aircraft annually.

Notes: The A-50 differs externally from the Il-76TD transport on which it is based primarily in having a 29.5-ft (9,00-m) rotodome on paired, inward-inclined pylons above the centre fuselage aft of the CG and large horizontal flat plate strakes on the aft part of the main undercarriage pods. Equipped with a flight refuelling probe immediately ahead of the flight deck, the A-50 may be operated in conjunction with the Il-78 *Midas* flight refuelling tanker derivative of the Il-76TD. Capable of detecting and tracking aircraft and cruise missiles flying at low altitude over land or water, it operates primarily with MiG-29, MiG-31 and Su-27 counterair fighters, tracking multiple targets and controlling multiple intercepts.

ILYUSHIN A-50 MAINSTAY

Dimensions: Span, 165 ft 8⅓ in (50,50 m); length, 152 ft 10¼ in (46,59 m); height, 48 ft 5¼ in (14,76 m); wing area, 3,229.2 sq ft (300,00 m²).

KAWASAKI T-4

Country of Origin: Japan.
Type: Tandem two-seat intermediate trainer.
Power Plant: Two 3,680 lb st (16.37 kN) Ishikawajima-Harima F3-IHI-30 turbofans.
Performance: Max speed (at 10,361 lb/4 700 kg), 645 mph (1 038 km/h) at sea level, 594 mph (956 km/h) at 36,000 ft (10 975 m); max continuous cruise (at 12,125 lb/5 500 kg), 495 mph (797 km/h); max initial climb (at 12,125 lb/5 500 kg), 10,000 ft/min (51 m/sec); range (max internal fuel), 806 mls (1 297 km), (with two 99 Imp gal/450 l drop tanks), 1,036 mls (1 668 km).
Weights: Empty, 8,157 lb (3 700 kg); max (design) take-off, 16,335 lb (7 500 kg).
Armament: (Weapons training) One 7,62-mm gun pod may be carried on centreline fuselage station and one AIM-9L Sidewinder AAM on each of two wing stations, or up to four 500-lb (227-kg) bombs.
Status: First of four XT-4 prototypes flown on 25 July 1985, with first production T-4 following on 28 June 1988, and production continuing at beginning of 1992 at approximately 24 annually against total Air Self-Defence Force requirement for 200 aircraft.
Notes: The T-4 has replaced both the Lockheed T-33A and the Fuji T-1 in the training syllabus of Japan's Air Self-Defence Force, and was developed jointly by Kawasaki (as prime contractor), Mitsubishi and Fuji. It was the first Japanese aircraft to combine a nationally-designed engine with an indigenous airframe for 25 years. An enhanced-capability version of the T-4 has been proposed to the Defence Agency as a replacement for the Mitsubishi T-2 advanced trainer.

Dimensions: Span, 32 ft 7$\frac{1}{2}$ in (9,94 m); length, 42 ft 8 in (13,00 m); height, 15 ft 1$\frac{1}{4}$ in (4,60 m); wing area, 226.05 sq ft (21,00 m²).

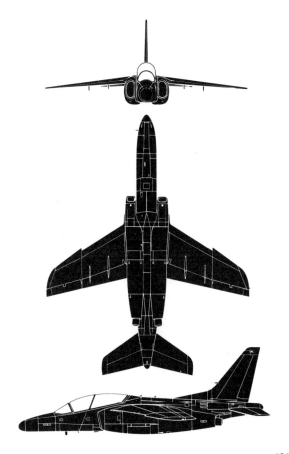

LEARJET 60

Country of Origin: USA.

Type: Light corporate executive transport.

Power Plant: Two 4,400 lb st (19,8 kN) Pratt & Whitney Canada PW305 turbofans.

Performance: (Maker's estimates) Max cruise speed, 533 mph (858 km/h); max operating altitude, 51,000 ft (15 550 m); max range (at long-range power at 44,000 ft/13 410 m with VFR reserves), 3,155 mls (5 075 km); typical range (four passengers and IFR reserves), 2,475 mls (3 980 km).

Weights: Max take-off, 22,750 lb (10 319 kg); (optional), 23,100 lb (10 478 kg).

Accommodation: Flight crew of two and typical passenger seating for six to nine in choice of interior layouts.

Status: Prototype (with Garrett TFE731 engines) Learjet 60 (modification of original Model 55 prototype) flown on 18 October 1990 as a proof-of-concept vehicle. Re-engined with PW305s and resumed flight testing on 13 June 1991. Definitive aerodynamic changes including enlarged Delta-Fins and extended wing root leading-edge introduced early 1992. Certification programme uses first three production aircraft, scheduled to fly in March, April and August 1992, to achieve certification in November. Deliveries to commence in the fourth quarter of 1992, with six aircraft scheduled for completion in 1992 and 15 in 1993.

Notes: The Model 60 is based upon the Model 55C, retaining the same wing, tail unit and 'Delta-Fins'. With an unchanged fuselage cross section, the Model 60 has a 43-in (109-cm) cabin stretch, improving passenger comfort and affording greater flexibility of interior design, approximately 28 in (71 cm) of this being added to the forward parallel section.

Dimensions: Span, 43 ft 9 in (13,34 m); length, 58 ft 8 in (17,88 m); height, 14 ft 8 in (4,47 m); wing area, 264·5 sq ft (24,57 m²).

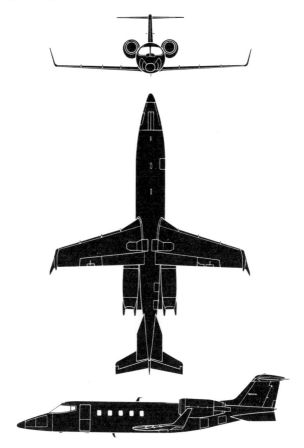

LET L 610

Country of Origin: Czechoslovakia.
Type: Short-haul regional transport.
Power Plant: Two 1,822 shp (1 358 kW) Motorlet M 602 or 1,870 shp (1,395 kW) General Electric CT7-9B turboprops.
Performance: (M 602) Max cruise speed, 304 mph (490 km/h) at 23,620 ft (7 200 m); range cruise, 253 mph (408 km/h) at 23,620 ft (7 200 m); max initial climb, 1,870 ft/min (9,5 m/sec); service ceiling, 33,630 ft (10 250 m); range with 45 min reserves, 540 mls (870 km) with max payload, 1,495 mls (2 406 km) with max fuel.
Weights: Operational empty, 19,841 lb (9 000 kg); max take-off, 30,865 lb (14 000 kg).
Accommodation: Crew of two and standard arrangement for 40 passengers four abreast. Alternative mixed passenger/cargo and all-cargo layouts available.
Status: First of three flying prototypes flown on 28 December 1988, followed by the second and third in 1991. Demonstration aircraft powered by CT7-9B engines expected to enter flight test early in 1992, with production of similarly-powered aircraft expected to start during that same year.
Notes: Designed primarily to meet a Soviet requirement for an aircraft to complement the 60-seat Il-114 regional airliner, the L 610 benefits from experience gained with the smaller L410. In order to increase the attractiveness of the aircraft on the Western market, the L610 is being offered with General Electric CT7-9B engines, with which it is anticipated that the L610 will obtain US certification in 1993. The L610 has been designed for soft-field operation and for the high descent rates demanded for landings at 'difficult' strips.

Dimensions: Span, 84 ft 0 in (25,60 m); length, 70 ft $3\frac{1}{4}$ in (21,42 m); height, 24 ft $11\frac{1}{2}$ in (7,61 m); wing area, 602·8 sq ft (56,00 m²).

LOCKHEED F-117A

Country of Origin: USA.

Type: Single-seat low-observable interdictor.

Power Plant: Two 10,800 lb st (48·0 kN) class General Electric F404-GE-F1D2 turbofans.

Performance: (Estimated) Max speed, 700 mph (1 126 km/h) at sea level, or Mach=0·92; normal max operating speed, 648 mph (1 043 km/h) at 5,000 ft (1 525 m), or Mach=0·87; normal cruise, 460 mph (740 km/h) at 30,000 ft (9 145 m).

Weights: (Estimated) Empty equipped, 30,000 lb (13 608 kg); max take-off, 52,500 lb (23 814 kg).

Armament: Up to 5,000 lb (2 270 kg) of ordnance accommodated by internal weapons bay, a typical load comprising two 2,000-lb (907-kg) laser-guided Mk 84 Paveway II bombs, GBU-10 or -27 laser-guided glide weapons, or AGM-65 Maverick or AGM-88 HARM air-to-surface missiles.

Status: First (pre-series) F-117A flown on 15 June 1981, with first delivery to the USAF mid 1982. Total of 59 ordered and produced at a rate of eight annually, with last being delivered 12 July 1990.

Notes: The F-117A is of unique, multi-faceted shape, its radical design affording low radar, infrared and optical signatures, and its primary role being that of defence suppression with internally-housed weaponry. Most aspects of the design were dictated by stealth considerations, and the F-117A is primarily of aluminium construction, both fuselage and wings being coated with several types of radar absorbent material. The entire fuselage surface consists of flat planes set in a limited number of alignments, the sharply swept (67 deg 30 min at leading edge) wing and the swept vee-type tail also being faceted. The turbofans are fed via rectangular overwing air intake grills and exhaust via narrow-slot 'platypus' rear-fuselage orifices. The F-117A equips two USAF squadrons.

LOCKHEED F-117A

Dimensions: Span, 43 ft 4 in (13,20 m); length, 65 ft 11 in (20,08 m); height, 12 ft 5 in (3,78 m); estimated wing area, 1,140 sq ft (105,9 m²).

LOCKHEED AC-130U HERCULES

Country of Origin: USA.

Type: Gunship.

Power Plant: Four 4,508 shp (3 362 kW) Allison T56-A-15 turboprops.

Performance: (Typical, at 155,000 lb/70 310 kg take-off weight) Max cruise, 374 mph (602 km/h); econ cruise, 345 mph (556 km/h); max initial climb, 1,900 ft/min (9,6 m/sec); service ceiling, 33,000 ft (10 060 m); range, up to 4,900 mls (7 885 km).

Weights: Max normal take-off, 155,000 lb (70 310 kg); max overload take-off, 175,000 lb (79 380 kg).

Accommodation: Crew of 13, including loaders. Two pilots, flight engineer and navigator on flight deck; battle management centre in cabin has seven monitoring consoles; observer stations in starboard side aft of flight deck and on rear ramp.

Armament: Three cannon in fuselage, all firing to port and comprising one 25-mm GAU-12/U six-barrel Gatling type, one 40-mm Bofors and one 105-mm howitzer.

Status: Twelve AC-130Us ordered by USAF from 1985 onwards, using new-build C-130H airframes from Lockheed at Marietta, converted at Palmdale by Rockwell. First flight (as bare C-130H) July 1988, and as first AC-130U conversion on 20 December 1990. Deliveries for operational use by 16th SOS to begin in 1993. The 2,000th C-130 (all versions) will be delivered in the second quarter of 1993.

Notes: The AC-130U is the latest Hercules gunship variant for the US Special Operations Force, which is also in process of introducing up to 27 MC-130H Combat Talon II deep penetration support transports. To replace upgraded AC-130Hs (photograph above), which will go to AFRes in place of AC-130As, the 'U-Boat' gunships have an extensive sensor suite and advanced fire-control radar system.

LOCKHEED AC-130U HERCULES

Dimensions: Span, 132 ft 7 in (40,41 m); length, 97 ft 9 in (29,79 m); height, 38 ft 3 in (11,66 m); wing area, 1,745.0 sq ft (162,12 m²).

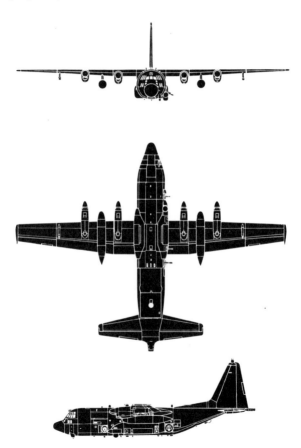

LOCKHEED P-3C ORION

Country of Origin: USA.
Type: Long-range maritime patrol aircraft.
Power Plant: Four 4,910 ehp (3 661 kW) Allison T56-A-14W turboprops.
Performance: Max speed (at 105,000 lb/47 625 kg), 473 mph (761 km/h) at 15,000 ft (4 570 m); econ cruise, 378 mph (608 km/h) at 25,000 ft (7 620 m); patrol speed, 237 mph (381 km/h) at 1,500 ft (457 m); max initial climb, 1,950 ft/min (9,9 m/sec); mission radius (three hours on station at 1,500 ft/457 m), 1,550 mls (2 494 km); max mission radius (at 135,000 lb/61 235 kg and no time on station), 2,383 mls (3 835 km).
Weights: Empty, 61,491 lb (27 890 kg); normal loaded, 135,000 lb (61 235 kg); max take-off, 142,000 lb (64 410 kg).
Accommodation: Normal crew of 10 comprising pilot, co-pilot, tactical co-ordinator, MAD operator, ordnance man, two acoustic sensor operators and a flight technician.
Armament: Eight Mk 54 depth bombs, eight 560-lb (254-kg) Mk 82 or 980-lb (444,5-kg) Mk 83 bombs, eight Mk 46 or six Mk 50 torpedoes internally and externally. Max total weapons load includes six 2,000-lb (907-kg) mines underwing and 7,252-lb (3 290-kg) internally.
Status: The first P-3C was flown on 18 September 1968 and orders for all versions totalled 650 aircraft at the beginning of 1992 when production in progress of eight P-3Ds for South Korea with deliveries scheduled for 1995.
Notes: The P-3 serves with Australia, Canada, Iran, Japan, Netherlands, New Zealand, Norway, Pakistan, Portugal and Spain, in addition to the USA, and licence manufacture is being undertaken in Japan, the Maritime Self-Defence Force of which is receiving 113 (107 P-3Cs, two UP-3Cs, three EP-3Es and one NP-3E). The P-3D is similar to the US Navy's P-3C Update III.

LOCKHEED P-3C ORION

Dimensions: Span, 99 ft 8 in (30,37 m); length, 116 ft 10 in (35,61 m); height, 33 ft 8½ in (10,29 m); wing area, 1,300 sq ft (120,77 m²).

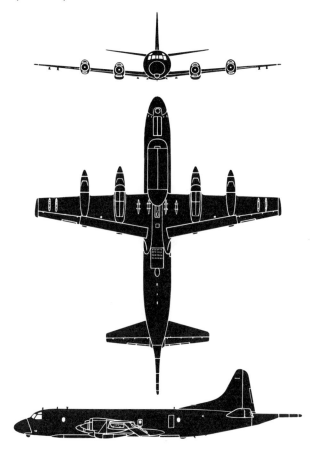

LOCKHEED YF-22

Country of Origin: USA.
Type: Single-seat air superiority fighter.
Power Plant: Two 35,000 lb st (156 kN) class Pratt & Whitney YF119-PW-100 variable-cycle turbofans.
Performance: (Estimated) Max speed, 915 mph (1 470 km/h) at low altitude, or Mach = 1·2, 1,190 mph (1 915 km/h) above 36,000 ft (10 975 m), or Mach = 1·8; max sustained cruise, 925–990 mph (1 490–1 595 km/h) above 36,000 ft (10 975 m), or Mach = 1·4–1·5; combat radius (internal fuel and full AAM armament), 800–900 mls (1 290–1 450 km).
Weights: (Estimated) Empty, 33,000 lb (14 970 kg); normal loaded, 60,000 lb (27 216 kg).
Armament: One 20-mm M61 rotary cannon and two short-range AIM-9 AAMs in centre weapons bay (of three in line abreast), with two AIM-120 medium-range AAMs in each of the outboard bays.
Status: First of two YF-22 prototypes (with General Electric YF120-GE-100 engines) flown on 29 September 1990, and second (with YF119 engines) flown on 30 October. Full-scale development covers nine YF-22As and two two-seat YF-22Bs, with first to fly in 1995. Production launch orders expected 1996 for service entry in 2000, with USAF planning to procure 648.
Notes: The YF-22, developed by Lockheed Aeronautical Systems teamed with General Dynamics and Boeing, was selected on 23 April 1991 by USAF to fulfil the Advanced Tactical Fighter (ATF) requirement. The FSD YF-22A will have a larger wing with a span of 44 ft 6 in (13,57 m), reduced length of 62 ft 6 in (19,06 m), enlarged tailplanes, smaller fins and changes to forward fuselage profile. US Navy will evaluate F-22 variants for its Advanced Tactical Fighter (F-14 replacement) and other potential applications.

LOCKHEED YF-22

Dimensions: Span, 43 ft 0 in (13,10 m); length, 64 ft 2 in (19,56 m); height, 17 ft 8$\frac{7}{8}$ in (5,40 m); wing area (estimated), 830 sq ft (77,1 m²).

McDONNELL DOUGLAS C-17A

Country of Origin: USA.

Type: Intra-theatre and long-range heavy-lift military freighter.

Power Plant: Four 41,700 lb st (185·5 kN) Pratt & Whitney F117-PW-100 turbofans.

Performance: (Manufacturer's estimates) Max cruise speed, 508 mph (818 km/h) at 36,000 ft (10 975 m), 403 mph (648 km/h) at low altitude; range (unrefuelled), 3,225 mls (5 190 km) with 129,200-lb (58 605-kg) payload, 3,110 mls (5 000 km) with 158,500-lb (71 895-kg) payload, 2,765 mls (4 445 km) with 167,000-lb (75 750-kg) payload.

Weights: (Projected) Operational empty, 269,000 lb (122 016 kg); max take-off, 580,000 lb (263 083 kg).

Accommodation: Normal flight crew of two plus a loadmaster. Main cargo hold able to accept three AH-64A helicopters or Army wheeled vehicles, including five-ton expandable vans in two side-by-side rows. Airdrop capability includes up to 102 paratroops, single platforms of up to 60,000 lb (27 215 kg), or multiple platforms of up to 110,000 lb (49 895 kg).

Status: Development C-17A first flown on 15 September 1991. First of initial batch of four production C-17As scheduled to join the flight test programme spring 1992. These will subsequently be delivered to the USAF for operational use. Total production of 120 C-17As for the USAF anticipated early 1992, with initial operational capability scheduled for 1993. Peak production target of 18 annually.

Notes: The C-17A is intended to provide intra-theatre and theatre airlift of outside loads, including armoured vehicles, directly into airfields in potential conflict areas. It is expected to be capable of operating from 3,000-ft (915-m) runways.

144

McDONNELL DOUGLAS C-17A

Dimensions: Span, 165 ft 0 in (50,29 m); length, 174 ft 0 in (53,04 m); height, 55 ft 1 in (16,79 m); wing area, 3,800 sq ft (353 m²).

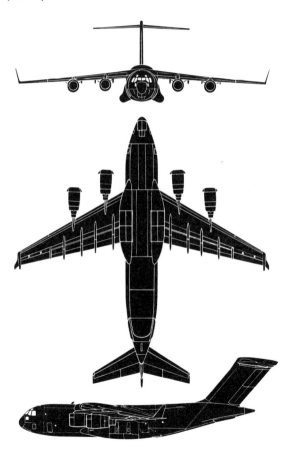

McDONNELL DOUGLAS F-15E EAGLE

Country of Origin: USA.

Type: Two-seat dual-role (air-air and air-ground) fighter.

Power Plant: Two 17,800 lb st (79.2kN) dry and 29,100 lb st (129.4 kN) afterburning Pratt & Whitney F100-PW-229 turbofans.

Performance: Max speed (short-endurance dash), 1,676 mph (2 698 km/h) at 40,000 ft (12 190 m), or Mach = 2·54, (sustained), 1,518 mph (2 443 km/h), or Mach = 2·3; max combat radius, 790 mls (1 270 km); max range (with conformal tanks and max external fuel), 2,765 mls (4 445 km).

Weights: Basic operational empty, 31,700 lb (14 379 kg); max take-off, 81,000 lb (36 741 kg).

Armament: One 20-mm six-barrel rotary cannon and max ordnance load of 24,500 lb (11 113 kg) on centreline and two wing stations plus four tangential carriers on conformal fuel tanks. For air-air mission up to four each AIM-7F/M Sparrow and AIM-9L/M Sidewinder AAMs, or up to eight AIM-120 AAMs may be carried.

Status: First production F-15E flown on 11 December 1986, with the last of 209 aircraft for the USAF to be delivered August 1993.

Notes: Evolved from the basic F-15 for long-range, deep interdiction air-ground missions by day or night, the F-15E embodies some 30 per cent airframe modifications. Initial F-15Es were powered by the 14,370 lb st (63.9 kN) dry and 23,450 lb st (104.3 kN) afterburning F100-PW 220 engines, but those delivered from August 1991 have the uprated -229 engines. The F-15E is the final production model of the Eagle for the USAF, the service having previously received 365 single-seat F-15As, 59 two-seat F-15Bs, 409 single-seat F-15Cs and 61 two-seat F-15Ds. A single-seat export version of the F-15E, the F-15F with limited air-ground capabilities, was being offered early in 1992.

McDONNELL DOUGLAS F-15E EAGLE

Dimensions: Span, 42 ft 9¾ in (13,05 m); length, 63 ft 9 in (19,43 m); height, 18 ft 5½ in (5,63 m); wing area, 608 sq ft (56,50 m²).

McDONNELL DOUGLAS F/A-18C HORNET

Country of Origin: USA.

Type: Single-seat shipboard and shore-based multi-role fighter.

Power Plant: Two 10,600 lb st (47·15 kN) dry and 15,800 lb st (70·27 kN) afterburning General Electric F404-GE-400 or 17,700 lb st (79 kN) afterburning F404-GE-402 turbofans.

Performance: (F404-GE-400) Max speed (AAMs on wingtip and fuselage stations), 1,190 mph (1 915 km/h) at 40,000 ft (12 150 m), or Mach = 1·8; combat radius (air-air mission), 480 mls (770 km), (with three 315 US gal/1 192 l drop tanks), 735 mls (1 180 km).

Weights: Empty, 23,050 lb (10 455 kg); loaded (air-air), 36,710 lb (16 651 kg), (attack), 49,224 lb (22 238 kg); max take-off, 56,000 lb (25 400 kg).

Armament: One 20-mm rotary cannon and up to 17,000 lb (7 711 kg) of ordnance/fuel distributed between nine stations.

Status: First of 11 development aircraft flown on 18 November 1978, with first production F/A-18A following in April 1980. Manufacture of 369 F/A-18As and 41 two-seat training F/A-18Bs for the US Navy and USMC followed by F/A-18C and two-seat F/A-18D in 1987, with 438 of the two versions (including all-weather and night attack, and recce versions of the latter) ordered for the two services.

Notes: All F/A-18Cs and Ds delivered from November 1989 have night and all-weather attack capability, and, from early 1992, the enhanced F404-GE-402 engine. Exports have comprised Australia (57 single-seaters and 18 two-seaters, all but two being licence built), Canada (98 single-seaters and 40 two-seaters) and Kuwait (32 single-seaters and eight two-seaters). The F/A-18D two-seater has supplanted the A-6 Intruder in the attack role in service with the US Marine Corps.

McDONNELL DOUGLAS F/A-18C HORNET

Dimensions: Span, 37 ft 6 in (11,43 m); length, 56 ft 0 in (17,07 m); height, 15 ft 4 in (4,67 m); wing area, 400 sq ft (37,16 m²).

McDONNELL DOUGLAS MD-11

Country of Origin: USA.

Type: Long-haul commercial transport.

Power Plant: Three 61,500 lb st (273·6 kN) General Electric CF6-80C2-D1F or 60,000 lb st (266·9 kN) Pratt & Whitney PW4460 turbofans.

Performance: (PW4460 engines) Max speed, 597 mph (962 km/h) at 27,000 ft (8 230 m), or Mach = 0·87; max cruise, 579 mph (932 km/h) at 30,000 ft (9 150 m); econ cruise, 544 mph (876 km/h) at 35,000 ft (10 670 m); max initial climb, 2,770 ft/min (14,07 m/sec); service ceiling, 32,600 ft (9 935 m); range (max payload with FAR international reserves), 5,760 mls (9 270 km).

Weights: Operational empty, 277,500 lb (125 874 kg); max take-off, 602,500 lb (273 289 kg); high gross weight option, 625,550 lb (283 750 kg).

Accommodation: Crew of two and max seating for 410 passengers 10 abreast, with a typical two-class arrangement for 323 passengers.

Status: First and second of five MD-11s used for flight test (and later refurbished for customer delivery) flew on 10 January and 1 March 1990 with CF6 engines, and third, with PW4460 engines, followed on 26 April. Certification of the CF6-engined version achieved on 8 November 1990, with first customer delivery (to Finnair) on 29 November and first revenue service on 20 December. Certification of PW version, 18 December 1990, for service entry with Delta Airlines. At the beginning of 1992, 172 firm orders (plus 160 other commitments) had been recorded, including 34 MD-11s delivered.

Notes: Three versions of the MD-11 are available: that described above, the MD-11CF Combi mixed passenger/cargo aircraft and the all-freight MD-11F.

McDONNELL DOUGLAS MD-11

Dimensions: Span, 169 ft 6 in (51,66 m); length, 200 ft 10 in (61,21 m); height, 57 ft 9 in (17,60 m); wing area, 3,648 sq ft (338,90 m²).

McDONNELL DOUGLAS MD-80

Country of Origin: USA.

Type: Short-to-medium-range jet transport.

Power Plant: Two (MD-81) 18,500 lb st (82.3 kN) Pratt & Whitney JT8D-209 turbofans with 750 lb st (3.3 kN) emergency reserve (ETR) or (MD-82) 20,000 lb st (89 kN) JT8D-217s with ETR of 850 lb st (3.8 kN) or (MD-83/88) 21,000 lb st (93.4 kN) JT8D-219s.

Performance: Max cruise, 550 mph (885 km/h) at 27,000 ft (8 230 m); range cruise, 505 mph (813 km/h) at 35,000 ft (10 670 m); range with 115 passengers (MD-81), 1,800 mls (2 896 km), (MD-82), 2,350 mls (3 778 km); (MD-83), 2,880 mls (4 635 km).

Weights: (MD-81): Operational empty, 78,420 lb (35 570 kg); max take-off, 140,000 lb (63 500 kg), (MD-83/88), 160,000 lb (72 575 kg).

Accommodation: Flight crew of two and up to 172 passengers five abreast.

Status: Three MD-80 development aircraft flown on 18 October and 6 December 1979 and 29 February 1980; MD-82 flown 8 January 1981, MD-83 flown 17 December 1984, MD-87 flown 4 December 1986, MD-88 flown 15 August 1987. Entry into service dates: MD-81 (Swissair), 5 October 1980; MD-82 (Republic), August 1982, MD-83 (Finnair) late 1985, MD-87 (Finnair and Austrian) late 1987, MD-88 (Delta) 5 January 1988. Totals of about 1,200 sales and 400 options/commitments for MD-80 variants by early 1992.

Notes: The MD-80 was launched as the DC-9 Super 80 in October 1977 as a stretched Srs 50. MD-81, 82, 83 and 88 are dimensionally similar, with differing engines, fuel options, avionics and weights. MD-87 (see 1991/92 edition) has a shorter fuselage.

McDONNELL DOUGLAS MD-80

Dimensions: Span, 107 ft 10 in (32,87 m); length, 147 ft 10 in (45,06 m); height, 29 ft 8 in (9.03 m); wing area, 1,270 sq ft (118 m²).

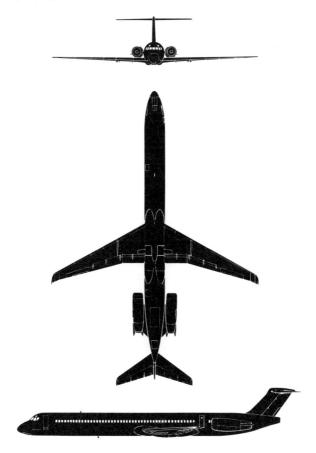

McDONNELL DOUGLAS MD-90

Country of Origin: USA.

Type: Short-to-medium haul commercial transport.

Power Plant: Two (-10) 22,000 lb st (97·86 kN) IAE V2522-D5 or (-30) 25,000 lb st (111.21 kN) V2525-D5 or (-40) 28,000 lb st (124.55 kN) V2528-D5 turbofans.

Performance: (Estimated) Cruising speed, 504 mph (811 km/h) at 35,000 ft (10 670 m); range (-10), 2,828 mls (4 551 km), (-30), 2,690 mls (4 329 km), (-40), 2,026 mls (3 261 km).

Weights: Operational empty (-10), 80,887 lb (36 690 kg), (-30), 86,588 lb (39 375 kg), (-40), 94,455 lb (42 844 kg), max take-off (-10), 139,000 lb (63,050 kg), (-30), 156,000 lb (70 760 kg); (-40), 163,500 lb (74 160 kg).

Accommodation: Flight crew of two. Typical two-class layouts for (-10) 114, (-30) 153 or (-40) 180 passengers.

Status: Programme launched 14 November 1989. First flight scheduled for first quarter of 1993, followed by deliveries (-30) late 1994, (-10) early 1995. Order for 95 plus 145 options announced by early 1992; launch customer, Delta Airlines.

Notes: MD-90 is a derivative of the MD-80, with V2500 engines in place of JT8Ds and several systems improvements. Variants differ in fuselage length and seating capacity: -10 has same length as MD-87 and -30 and -40 have extra lengths of 22 ft 2 in (6,76 m) and 41 ft 2 in (12,55 m) respectively. The -30T is a 'Trunkliner' proposal for China, with dual tandem landing gear for the Chinese domestic airfields, and the -50 is a long-range version of the -30 with more fuel and higher weights. The -20 designation is reserved for possible conversions of MD-80s to have V2500 engines. MD-95 is a proposed MD-80 derivative with Rolls-Royce Tay engines.

McDONNELL DOUGLAS MD-90

Dimensions: Span, 107 ft 10 in (32,87 m); length (-10), 130 ft 5 in (39,75 m), (-30), 152 ft 7 in (46,51 m), (-40), 171 ft 7 in (52,30 m); height, 30 ft 6 in (9,30 m); wing area, 1,209 sq ft (112,32 m²).

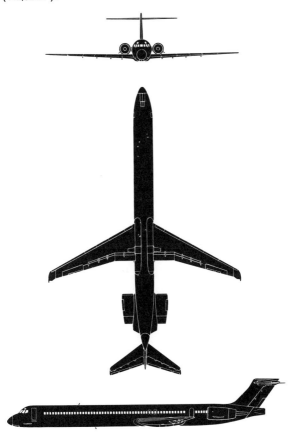

McDONNELL DOUGLAS/BRITISH AEROSPACE
T-45A GOSHAWK

Countries of Origin: USA and United Kingdom.

Type: Tandem two-seat carrier-capable basic/advanced trainer.

Power Plant: One 5,840 lb st (25·98 kN) Rolls-Royce/Turbo-méca F405-RR-401 (Adour Mk 871) turbofan.

Performance: Max speed, 620 mph (997 km/h) at 8,000 ft (2 440 m), 573 mph (922 km/h) at 30,000 ft (9 150 m); max initial climb, 6,982 ft/min (35,47 m/sec); time to 30,000 ft (9 150 m), 7·2 min; service ceiling, 42,250 ft (12 880 m); ferry range (internal fuel only), 1,150 mls (1 850 km).

Weights: (Estimated) Empty, 9,399 lb (4 263 kg); max take-off, 12,758 lb (5 787 kg).

Armament: Provision for one stores pylon beneath each wing for rocket pods, practice multiple bomb racks, etc, plus fuselage centreline pylon.

Status: First of two full-scale engineering development T-45As flown on 16 April 1988, with first production standard aircraft flown on 16 December 1991 and delivered to US Navy on 23 January 1992 against a requirement for 268 aircraft. Flight testing was scheduled to be completed mid 1992.

Notes: The T-45A Goshawk has been derived from the British Aerospace Hawk as part of an integrated training system embodying aircraft, academics, simulators and logistics support. Seventy-six per cent of the manufacture of the T-45A is being undertaken in the USA, and significant changes include a new undercarriage, an arrester hook, introduction of full-span slats, redesigned speed brakes, a more powerful engine, a ventral fin and airframe strengthening. Some 60 per cent of the internal structure differs from that of the Hawk.

McDONNELL DOUGLAS/BRITISH AEROSPACE T-45A GOSHAWK

Dimensions: Span, 30 ft 9¾ in (9,39 m); length (including probe), 39 ft 3⅛ in (11,97 m); height, 13 ft 5 in (4,09 m); wing area, 179·64 sq ft (16,69 m²).

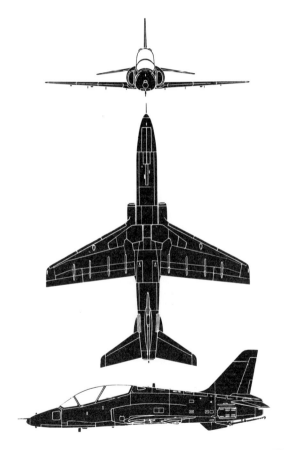

McDONNELL DOUGLAS TAV-8B HARRIER II

Countries of Origin: USA and United Kingdom.

Type: Tandem two-seat V/STOL conversion trainer.

Power Plant: One 21,450 lb st (95·42 kN) Rolls-Royce F402-RR-406A (Pegasus 11-21) vectored-thrust turbofan.

Performance: Max speed, 667 mph (1 074 km/h) at sea level, or Mach = 0·87, 587 mph (945 km/h) at 36,000 ft (10 975 m), or Mach = 0·9; ferry range (with two 300 US gal/1 136 l external tanks retained), 1,647 mls (2 650 km).

Weights: Operational empty (including pilot), 14,223 lb (6 451 kg); max take-off (for STO), 29,750 lb (13 495 kg).

Armament: (Weapons training) Two underwing stores stations which can carry up to three Mk 76 practice bombs or an LAU-68 rocket launcher.

Status: First TAV-8B flown on 21 October 1986, with initial deliveries to the US Marine Corps commencing August 1987, and 24 procured by the service. The first of two was supplied to the Italian Navy on 23 August 1991, and two are to be procured by the Spanish Navy. Thirteen essentially similar aircraft ordered for the RAF in February 1990 as Harrier T Mk 10s.

Notes: The TAV-8B is a two-seat derivative of the AV-8B single-seat close support aircraft. The latter serves with the US Marine Corps and the Spanish Navy (as the EAV-8B Matador II), and is operated by the RAF as the Harrier GR Mks 5 and 7 (which see). The TAV-8B differs in forward fuselage and vertical tail, and the RAF's Harrier T Mk 10 equivalent (illustrated opposite) has forward-looking infrared and night vision systems. Of 256 AV-8Bs ordered for the USMC, the 167th and subsequent 61 have night attack capability and the final 24 are to be delivered to Harrier II Plus standard with multimode radar and increased thrust. The Italian Navy is to receive 16 Harrier II Plus aircraft, the USMC hopes to rebuild 114 earlier aircraft to the same standard and Spain plans to rebuild 11 EAV-8Bs and acquire eight new-build aircraft.

Dimensions: Span, 30 ft 4 in (9,24 m); length, 50 ft 3 in (15,32 m); height, 13 ft 4¾ in (4,08 m); wing area (including LERX), 238·7 sq ft (22,18 m²).

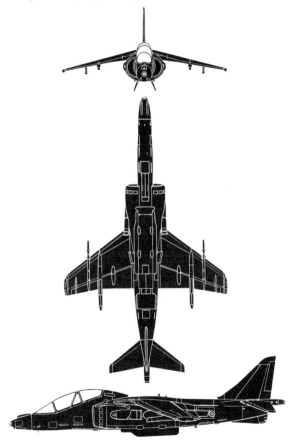

MIKOYAN MIG-29 (FULCRUM)

Country of Origin: Commonwealth of Independent States (Russia).

Type: Single-seat counterair fighter.

Power Plant: Two 11,110 lb st (49·4 kN) dry and 18,298 lb st (81·4 kN) afterburning NPO Klimov (St Petersburg) RD-33 turbofans.

Performance: Max speed (with four R-27 and two R-73 AAMs), 805 mph (1 300 km/h) at sea level, or Mach = 1·06, 1,518 mph (2 445 km/h) at 39,370 ft (12 000 m), or Mach = 2·3; max initial climb, 64,960 ft/min (330 m/sec); service ceiling, 55,775 ft (17 000 m); range (internal fuel), 932 mls (1 500 km), (with max external fuel), 1,802 mls (2 900 km).

Weights: Loaded, 33,598 lb (15 240 kg); max take-off, 40,785 lb (18 500 kg).

Armament: One 30-mm GSh-301 cannon plus six medium-range R-27T and R (*Alamo-A* and *-B*) medium-range AAMs, or mix of R-27 and R-73 (*Aphid*) short-range AAMs distributed between six wing stations, or up to 6,614 lb (3 000 kg) of air-to-ground ordnance.

Status: First of 19 prototypes flown on 6 October 1977, with service deliveries commencing 1983 and export deliveries following (India and Syria) in 1987. Supplied to a dozen countries, some 700 had been produced by mid 1992 when production was (subject to further export orders) phasing out.

Notes: The *Fulcrum-A* version of the MiG-29 is illustrated above and the *Fulcrum-C* with raised dorsal fairing is illustrated opposite. *Fulcrum-B* (MiG-29UB) is a tandem two-seat combat trainer and *Fulcrum-D* (MiG-29K) is an experimental shipboard version with arrester gear, folding outer wing panels, flight refuelling equipment and a modified undercarriage. The MiG-29M, prototype trials of which were completed in 1991, is a more advanced model with a 'glass' cockpit, fly-by-wire control system and more powerful RD-33K engines.

Dimensions: Span, 37 ft $3\frac{1}{4}$ in (11,36 m); length (including probe), 56 ft $9\frac{7}{8}$ in (17,32 m); height, 15 ft $6\frac{1}{4}$ in (4,73 m); wing area, 409·04 sq ft (38,00 m²).

MIKOYAN MIG-31 (FOXHOUND)

Country of Origin: Commonwealth of Independent States (Russia).

Type: Tandem two-seat all-weather interceptor fighter.

Power Plant: Two 34,170 lb st (151·9 kN) afterburning MKB (Soloviev) D-30F-6 turbofans.

Performance: Max speed (short-endurance dash), 1,868 mph (3 006 km/h) above 36,100 ft (11 000 m), or Mach = 2·8, (sustained), 1,551 mph (2 496 km/h), or Mach = 2·35; time to 32,810 ft (10 000 m), 7·9 min; endurance (with two 550 Imp gal/ 1 500 l external tanks), 3·6 hrs; tactical radius, 870 mls (1 400 km) at Mach = 0·85.

Weights: Loaded (internal fuel only), 90,388 lb (41 000 kg); max take-off, 101,852 lb (46 200 kg).

Armament: One 23-mm multi-barrel GSh-6-23 cannon and up to eight R-33 (*Amos*) long-range AAMs (four in tandem pairs on fuselage centreline and two on each of two wing pylons), or four R-33 and four R-60 (*Aphid*) short-range AAMs.

Status: First prototype (Ye-155MP) flown on 16 September 1975, with series production initiated in 1979, followed by service entry late 1982. Production continuing mid 1992 at Nizhny-Novgorod (formerly Gorkiy).

Notes: Evolved from the 'sixties technology MiG-25, but possessing no commonality with the earlier aircraft, the MiG-31 was developed around a large phased-array radar and an associated weapon system embodying lookdown/shootdown and multiple-target engagement capability. The MiG-31 is usually deployed in a four-aircraft formation with radars interconnected by on-board data links and permitting areas of 500–560 mls (800–900 km) width to be swept. The MiG-31M (*Foxhound-B*) is an improved version (see opposite) embodying minor aerodynamic changes and upgraded equipment.

MIKOYAN MIG-31 (FOXHOUND)

Dimensions: Span, 44 ft 2 in (13,46 m); length (including probe), 74 ft $5\frac{1}{4}$ in (22,69 m); height, 20 ft $2\frac{1}{8}$ in (6,15 m); wing area, 663·08 sq ft (61,60 m²).

NAMC K-8

Country of Origin: China.
Type: Tandem two-seat basic trainer and light ground attack aircraft.
Power Plant: One 3,600 lb st (16·0 kN) Garrett TFE731-2A-2A turbofan.
Performance: Max speed, 497 mph (800 km/h) at sea level; max initial climb, 5,315 ft/min (27 m/sec); service ceiling, 43,600 ft (13 290 m); range with 15 per cent reserves (internal fuel), 924 mls (1 487 km), (two 55 Imp gal/250 l drop tanks), 1,398 mls (2 250 km) at 330 mph (530 km/h).
Weights: Empty equipped, 5,637 lb (2 557 kg); loaded (clean), 7,716 lb (3 500 kg); max take-off, 9,259 lb (4 200 kg).
Armament: (Attack) One 23-mm cannon pod on fuselage centreline with four underwing stations for rocket or gun pods, bombs or missiles.
Status: First of three flying prototypes flown on 21 November 1990 with the remaining two having joined the test programme by early 1992. The first of 15 pre-production aircraft was scheduled to enter flight tests in July 1992.
Notes: The K-8, also known as the Karakorum 8, has been developed independently by NAMC (Nanchang Aircraft Manufacturing Company). The Pakistan Aeronautical Complex has contributed maintenance and operational expertise, the K-8 adhering closely to a requirement for a basic trainer formulated by the Pakistan Air Force. It is anticipated that, subject to the successful completion of Pakistan Air Force service evaluation, partially-equipped K-8 airframes will be delivered to the Pakistan Aeronautical Complex at Kamra for completion, this establishment eventually being responsible for manufacture of approximately 25 per cent of the airframe. At the time of closing for press, no order for the K-8 had been placed on behalf of the People's Republic of China Air Force.

Dimensions: Span, 31 ft 7¼ in (9,63 m); length (including probe), 38 ft 0¾ in (11,60 m); height, 13 ft 9¾ in (4,21 m); wing area, 183·5 sq ft (17,05 m²).

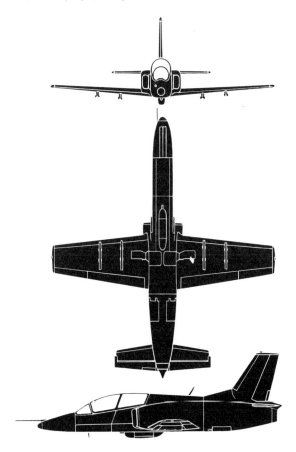

NORTHROP B-2

Country of Origin: USA.

Type: Low-observable strategic penetration bomber.

Power Plant: Four 19,000 lb st (84·5 kN) General Electric F118-GE-110 turbofans.

Performance: Max speed (estimated), 595–628 mph (955–1 010 km/h) at 50,000 ft (15 240 m), or Mach = 0·9–0·95; range (with eight AGM-69 SRAMs or AGM-129 ACMs and eight B83 free-fall bombs), 7,255 mls (11 675 km) HI-HI-HI, 5,067 mls (8 154 km) HI-LO-HI; unrefuelled range, 7,255 mls (11 675 km); service ceiling, 50,000 ft (15 240 m).

Weights: Empty, 100,000–110,000 lb (45 360–49 900 kg); normal loaded weight, 371,330 lb (168 433 kg); max take-off, 400,000 lb (181 437 kg).

Armament: Rotary launcher in each of two side-by-side weapons bays for maximum of 16 AGM-69 SRAMs (Short-Range Attack Missiles) or AGM-129 ACMs (Advanced Cruise Missiles). Alternative weapons include B61 and B83 free-fall nuclear bombs, 1,000-lb (453,6-kg) Mk 36 sea mines, or up to 80 500-lb (227-kg) Mk 82 bombs.

Status: The first of five full-scale development B-2s was flown on 17 July 1989, the second and third following on 19 October 1990 and 18 June 1991. The second B-2 is to remain a test aircraft and the remaining four are to be refurbished for delivery to the USAF. At the time of closing for press it appeared that procurement would be restricted to a further 15 aircraft.

Notes: Possessing a crew of two, the B-2 is largely of composite construction, some structures being laminates of composites and metals. The mission of the B-2 was redefined by the USAF early 1992, emphasis being transferred from nuclear to conventional operations.

NORTHROP B-2

Dimensions: Span, 172 ft 0 in (52,43 m); length, 69 ft 0 in (21,03 m); height, 17 ft 0 in (5,18 m).

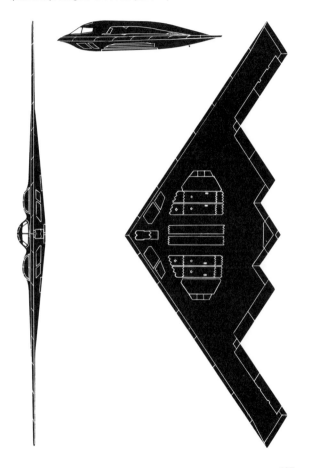

PACIFIC AEROSPACE CT-4C TURBINE AIRTRAINER

Country of Origin: New Zealand.

Type: Light primary trainer.

Power Plant: One 420 shp (313 kW) Allison 250-B17D turboprop.

Performance: (Manufacturer's estimates) Max level speed, 236 mph (380 km/h) at sea level, 239 mph (385 km/h) at 10,000 ft (3 050 m), 224 mph (361 km/h) at 20,000 ft (6 100 m); cruising speed, 190 mph (306 km/h); max initial climb, 2,765 ft/min (14,0 m/sec); range (no reserves), 718 mls (1 156 km) at 10,000 ft (3 050 m).

Weights: Max take-off, 2,650 lb (1 202 kg).

Accommodation: Instructor and student pilot side-by-side.

Status: Prototype (AESL CT-4A) first flown on 23 February 1972. Total of 96 built by 1977 included 24 for the Royal Thai AF, 51 for RAAF and 19 (CT-4B) for RNZAF. Pacific Aerospace acquired design rights in January 1982 and continued with design of CT-4C turboprop variant. Prototype CT-4C (conversion of a damaged RNZAF CT-4B airframe) first flown 21 January 1991. Production of 12 CT-4Bs for BAe-Ansett Flying College completed by PAC in September 1991.

Notes: Original CT-4A was developed in New Zealand as military trainer, based on Victa Airtourer, which was built in Australia to the designs of Henry Millicer. CT-4A and CT-4B (latter with higher gross weight and RNZAF-specified avionics) powered by 210 hp Teledyne Continental IO-360-H piston engine. A derivative of the CT-4C is proposed with a retractable undercarriage as the CT-4CR, and the CT-4E, flown in 1991, is a variant of the CT-4B proposed for the USAF Enhanced Flight Screener requirement.

Dimensions: Span, 26 ft 0 in (7,92 m); length, 23 ft 5 in (7,14 m); height, 8 ft 6 in (2,59 m); wing area, 129·0 sq ft (11,98 m²).

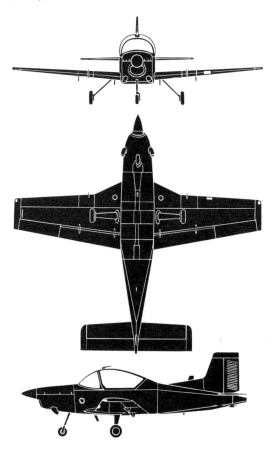

PANAVIA TORNADO F MK 3

Country of Origin: United Kingdom.
Type: Tandem two-seat air defence fighter.
Power Plant: Two 9,100 lb st (40·5 kN) dry and 16,520 lb st (73·5 kN) afterburning Turbo-Union RB199-34R Mk 104 turbofans.
Performance: Max speed, 920 mph (1 480 km/h) at low altitude, or Mach = 1·2, 1,450 mph (2 333 km/h) at 40,000 ft (12 190 m), or Mach = 2·2; time to 30,000 ft (9 145 m), 1·7 min; tactical radius (combat air patrol with two 330 Imp gal/1 500 l drop tanks and 2 hrs loiter allowance), 350–450 mls (560–725 km); ferry range (with four 330 Imp gal/1 500 l external tanks), 2,650 mls (4 265 km).
Weights: Approx operational empty, 31,970 lb (14 500 kg); max take-off, 61,700 lb (27 986 kg).
Armament: One 27-mm cannon plus four Sky Flash medium-range and four AIM-9L Sidewinder short-range AAMs.
Status: First of three F Mk 2 prototypes flown on 27 October 1979, followed by first of 18 production F Mk 2s (including six dual-control F Mk 2Ts) on 5 March 1984. Production switched to F Mk 3 with initial flight of 20 November 1985 and deliveries commencing July 1986. Total of 173 (including F Mk 2s) delivered to the RAF, and 24 similar aircraft supplied to the Royal Saudi Air Force.
Notes: The Tornado F Mk 3 is the definitive air defence version (ADV) for the RAF of the multi-national (UK, Federal Germany and Italy) Tornado interdictor strike (IDS) aircraft. An electronic combat and reconnaissance (ECR) version of the IDS Tornado has been developed for Germany's *Luftwaffe*.

Dimensions: Span (25 deg sweep), 45 ft $7\frac{1}{4}$ in (13,90 m), (68 deg sweep), 28 ft $2\frac{1}{2}$ in (8,59 m); length, 59 ft $3\frac{7}{8}$ in (18,08 m); height, 18 ft $8\frac{1}{2}$ in (5,70 m); wing area, 286·3 sq ft (26,60 m²).

171

PIAGGIO P.180 AVANTI

Country of Origin: Italy.

Type: Light corporate transport.

Power Plant: Two 1,485 shp (1 107 km/h) Pratt & Whitney Canada PT6A-66 turboprops flat-rated to 850 shp (634 kW).

Performance: Max speed, 455 mph (732 km/h) at 28,300 ft (8 625 m); max continuous cruise, 400 mph (644 km/h) at 39,000 ft (11 885 m); max initial climb, 2,870 ft/min (14,9 m/sec); service ceiling, 41,000 ft (12 495 m); range at 39,000 ft (11 890 m) with IFR reserves, 1,638 mls (2 637 km) and with VFR reserves, 1,980 mls (3 187 km).

Weights: Empty equipped, 7,460 lb (3 384 kg); max take-off, 11,200 lb (5 080 kg).

Accommodation: Pilot and co-pilot/passenger on flight deck with seating in main cabin for up to nine passengers. Standard configuration for seven passengers in individual seats.

Status: Two prototypes flown on 23 September 1986 and 15 May 1987, with first production aircraft flying on 29 January 1990. Full certification obtained on 2 October 1990. Four series Avantis had been delivered by the beginning of 1991, in which year a further 10 aircraft were produced. Production rate, up to two a month in 1992.

Notes: The configurationally-innovative Avanti is marketed in the US by the wholly-owned subsidiary Piaggio Aviation Inc. The latter receives its aircraft from Duncan-Piaggio Aviation in Lincoln, Nebraska, where 'green' aircraft from Piaggio in Italy are completed and flight tested.

PIAGGIO P.180 AVANTI

Dimensions: Span, 46 ft $0\frac{1}{2}$ in (14,03 m); length, 47 ft $3\frac{1}{2}$ in (14,41 m); height, 12 ft 11 in (3,94 m); wing area, 172·22 sq ft (16,00 m²).

PILATUS PC-9

Country of Origin: Switzerland.
Type: Tandem two-seat basic/advanced trainer.
Power Plant: One 1,150 shp (857 kW) Pratt & Whitney Canada PT6A-62 turboprop flat-rated at 950 shp (708 kW).
Performance: (At 4,960 lb/2 250 kg) Max speed, 311 mph (500 km/h) at sea level, 345 mph (556 km/h) at 20,000 ft (6 100 m); max initial climb rate, 4,090 ft/min (20,8 m/sec); max range (five per cent fuel reserve plus 20 min), 1,020 mls (1 642 km) at 25,000 ft (7 620 m).
Weights: Basic empty, 3,715 lb (1 685 kg); max take-off (aerobatic), 4,960 lb (2 250 kg), (utility), 7,055 lb (3 200 kg).
Status: First and second prototypes flown on 7 May and 20 July 1984, with first production deliveries late 1985, with some 175 ordered by beginning of 1992. Customers comprise Angola (4), Australia (67), Cyprus (2), Germany (10), Iraq (20), Mexico (10), Myanmar (4), Saudi Arabia (30), Switzerland (4), Thailand (20), USA (3).
Notes: PC-9s supplied to Saudi Arabia have cockpit instrumentation compatible with that of the BAe Hawk, and Australian aircraft (PC-9As) have EFIS and low-pressure tyres as standard. Two of the Australian aircraft were delivered flyaway, six as kits, 11 as major components for assembly by Hawker de Havilland and ASTA, and the remaining 48 were manufactured by these companies. Those delivered to Germany (PC-9Bs) are operated as target tugs by a private company on behalf of the *Luftwaffe*. The four supplied to the Swiss *Flugwaffe* fulfil target presentation and target-towing tasks.

Dimensions: Span, 33 ft 2½ in (10,12 m); length, 33 ft 4¾ in (10,17 m); height, 10 ft 8⅓ in (3,26 m); wing area, 175·3 sq ft (16,29 m²).

PILATUS PC-12

Country of Origin: Switzerland.

Type: Light utility and business transport.

Power Plant: One 1,200 shp (895 kW) Pratt & Whitney Canada PT6A-67B turboprop (flat rated from 1,780 shp (1 327 kW)).

Performance: (Manufacturer's estimates) Max cruise speed, 309 mph (497 km/h) at 25,000 ft (7 620 m); max initial climb, 2,050 ft/min (10,40 m/sec); max operating altitude, 25,000 ft (7 620 m); max range (45 min reserves), 1,843 mls (2 966 km).

Weights: Empty (freighter), 4,813 lb (2 183 kg), (passenger configuration), 5,260 lb (2 386 kg); max take-off, 8,818 lb (4 000 kg).

Accommodation: Pilot and co-pilot/passenger on flight deck and up to nine passengers in individual seats for commuter role, or six seats in executive version.

Status: First of two prototypes entered flight test on 31 May 1991, with the second planned for mid-1992 and first customer deliveries in fourth quarter 1993 following Swiss certification in mid-year and US certification late-1993. Options on more than 30 by early 1992. First production batch of 35 aircraft launched by company board decision March 1992.

Notes: The PC-12 is a pressurised multi-role transport, the multiple mission capabilities ranging from executive level transportation to long-distance delivery of freight and oversized equipment. Variants on offer include the PC-12 Combi which, able to carry four passengers in the main cabin, offers 210 cu ft (5,95 m³) of space for freight. The passenger and pure freight versions are known as the PC-12P and PC-12F respectively.

Dimensions: Span, 45 ft $2\frac{1}{2}$ in (13,78 m); length, 45 ft $9\frac{1}{2}$ in (13,96 m); height, 13 ft 7 in (4,14 m); wing area, 243·3 sq ft (22,6 m²).

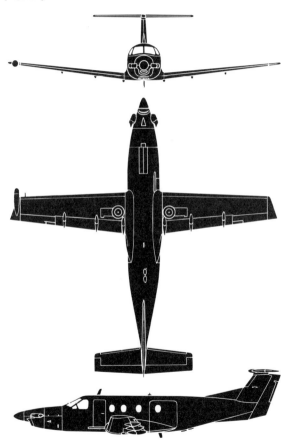

PILATUS BRITTEN-NORMAN DEFENDER 4000

Country of Origin: United Kingdom.
Type: Light multi-role military transport and surveillance.
Power Plant: Two 475 shp (354 kW) Allison 250 B17F turbo-props, each derated to 400 shp (299 kW).
Performance: Max speed, 225 mph (363 km/h); transit speed, 178 mph (287 km/h); maritime patrol speed, 150 mph (240 km/h); max initial climb, 1,250 ft/min (6,35 m/sec); loiter endurance, more than 6 hrs.
Weights: Empty equipped, 4,300 lb (1 950 kg); max take-off, 8,500 lb (3 855 kg).
Armament: Four wing hardpoints stressed for 750 lb (340 kg) each inboard and 360 lb (159 kg) outboard, with standard NATO pylons and pick-ups for a variety of stores or sensor pods.
Accommodation: Minimum crew, one pilot and one operator. Normal crew, two pilots and one or two operators. Up to nine passengers in transport role.
Status: Demonstrator BN-2T2 flown early 1991 in basic configuration, modified later in 1991 by Westinghouse Electric in US as multi-sensor surveillance aircraft (MSSA) with AN/APG-66 360-deg scan radar in nose and WF-360 IR imaging system under cabin. First MSSA leased to US Navy for test-pilot training on sensor systems at Patuxent River, 1992.
Notes: Defender 4000 is latest derivative of basic BN-2T Turbine Islander and Defender, featuring uprated engines and increased wing span to permit operation at higher gross weights, expected eventually to reach 10,000 lb (4 536 kg). Fuel capacity is increased and the structure strengthened. Provision is made for a variety of sensors and other equipment to suit the aircraft for AEW, ELINT, border patrol, etc, as well as maritime surveillance in the MSSA version (illustrated above).

PILATUS BRITTEN-NORMAN DEFENDER 4000

Dimensions: Span, 53 ft 0 in (16,15 m); length, 40 ft 7¼ in (12,37 m); height, 13 ft 8¾ in; wing area, 337 sq ft (31,30 m²).

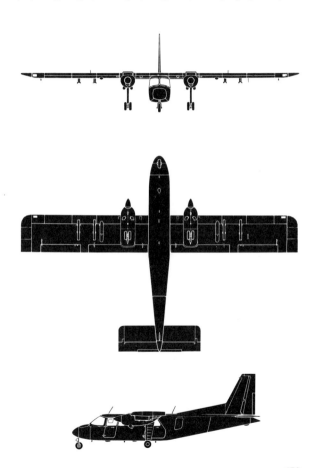

PZL-130T TURBO ORLIK

Country of Origin: Poland.
Type: Tandem two-seat basic and multi-purpose trainer.
Power Plant: One (PZL-130TB) 751 shp (560 kW) Walter M 601T or (PZL-130TC) 950 shp (708 kW) Pratt & Whitney Canada PT6A-62 turboprop.
Performance: (PZL-130TC) Max speed, 316 mph (508 km/h) at sea level, 348 mph (560 km/h) at 20,000 ft (6 095 m); max initial climb, 4,055 ft/min (20,6 m/sec); max range (internal fuel), 578 mls (930 km) at sea level, (with two 75 Imp gal/340 l drop tanks), 1,429 mls (2 300 km).
Weights: (PZL-130TC) Empty equipped, 3,197 lb (1 450 kg); max loaded (aerobatic), 4,409 lb (2 000 kg); max take-off, 5,952 lb (2 700 kg).
Status: First Turbo Orlik (conversion of third piston-engined PZL-130 Orlik) was flown on 13 July 1986 with a PT6A engine, and second flew on 12 January 1989 with an M-601E engine. A third Turbo Orlik flew on 18 September 1991, and initial batch of 12 ordered for the Deblin Flying Training Academy (but deliveries uncertain mid 1992) against total Polish Air Force requirement for 48 aircraft.
Notes: Derived from the piston-engined PZL-130 Orlik (Eaglet) which did not proceed further than prototype (four) stage, the Turbo Orlik is currently offered in several versions. It is anticipated that the version for the Polish Air Force will have either the M 601E or T turboprop (see 1991/92 edition). Both the M 601-powered PZL-130TB and PT6A-powered PZL-130TC have a longer span wing than the 26 ft 3 in (8,00 m) wing of the first prototypes, this having double-slotted flaps. These versions have ejection seats, more powerful brakes and nosewheel steering. The proposed PZL-130TD and TE have the 750 shp PT6A-25C and 550 shp PT6A-25 engine respectively.

Dimensions: Span, 29 ft 6⅓ in (9,00 m); length, 29 ft 6⅓ in (9,00 m); height, 11 ft 7 in (3,53 m); wing area, 139·93 sq ft (13,00 m²).

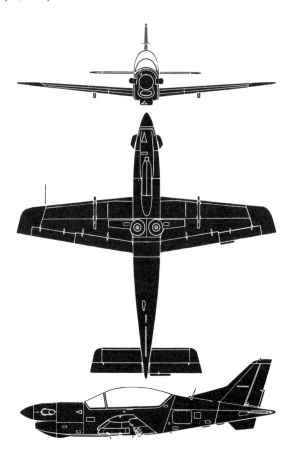

PZL I-22 IRYDA

Country of Origin: Poland.

Type: Tandem two-seat advanced trainer and light close support aircraft.

Power Plant: Two 2,425 lb st (10·79 kN) PZL Rzeszów SO-3W22 turbojets.

Performance: Max speed, 568 mph (915 km/h) at sea level; max cruise, 574 mph (924 km/h) at 32,810 ft (10 000 m); max initial climb, 7,283 ft/min (37 m/sec); service ceiling, 41,340 ft (12 600 m); range (internal fuel), 1,037 mls (1 670 km).

Weights: Operational empty, 8,735 lb (3 962 kg); max take-off, 16,519 lb (7 493 kg).

Armament: One 23-mm GSh-23L twin-barrel cannon in fuselage centreline pack and four wing stations each stressed for ordnance loads of 1,102 lb (500 kg).

Status: First of five prototypes flown on 3 March 1985, with last joining the test programme during 1990. Twelve pre-series aircraft similar to the prototypes scheduled to undergo service evaluation. Polish Air Force requirement for total of 80 aircraft with western avionics and more powerful engines (including pre-series aircraft which will be upgraded).

Notes: The Iryda (Iridium) has undergone protracted development and current planning calls for adoption of Iryda 93 standards for aircraft subsequent to the pre-series. The Iryda 93 is to have Bendix-King avionics and more powerful engines, these possibly being IL K-15 turbojets of 3,305 lb st (14·7 kN). Alternative engines under consideration are the Rolls-Royce Viper, the SNECMA Larzac and an unspecified Pratt & Whitney unit. A single-seat light strike version of the Iryda, the I-22MS, was under development at the beginning of 1992.

PZL I-22 IRYDA

Dimensions: Span, 31 ft 6 in (9,60 m); length, 43 ft 4½ in (13,22 m); height, 14 ft 1¼ in (4,30 m); wing area, 214·4 sq ft (19,92 m²).

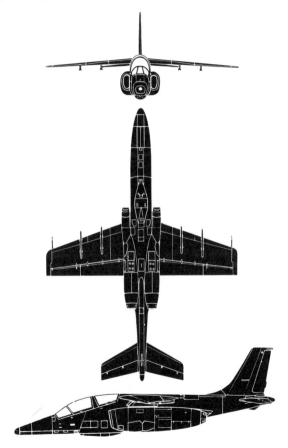

PZL-105 FLAMING

Country of Origin: Poland.

Type: Light multi-purpose aircraft.

Power Plant: One (PZL-105M) 360 hp (268·5 kW) Vedeneyev M-14P nine-cylinder air-cooled radial or (PZL-105L) 400 hp (298 kW) Textron Lycoming IO-720-A1B eight-cylinder horizontally-opposed air-cooled engine.

Performance (PZL-105M, estimated): Max speed, 163 mph (262 km/h); max cruise, 133 mph (214 km/h); economical cruise, 121 mph (195 km/h); max initial climb, 1,710 ft/min (8,7 m/sec); max range, 614 mls (989 km) at max cruise, 720 mls (1 159 km) at economical cruise.

Weights (PZL-105M): Equipped empty, 2,425 lb (1 100 kg); max take-off, 4,078 lb (1 850 kg).

Accommodation: Pilot and up to five passengers, including one alongside pilot, with option for dual controls.

Status: First of three prototypes, a PZL-105M, flown on 19 December 1989. Second prototype, a PZL-105L, flown in summer 1991. Initial certification expected in 1992, with series PZL-105Ls available in 1993.

Notes: The Flaming (Flamingo) was at first identified as the Wilga 88, but it shared little but general configuration with the long-serving PZL-104 Wilga (Oriole) family, and was essentially an all-new design planned as a Wilga replacement. Some 900 Wilgas had been built by the time the Flaming entered initial flight trials. To be certificated to the US FAR Part 23 standard, the Flaming is intended to operate in a wide range of roles, and a floatplane version is planned.

Dimensions: Span, 41 ft 8 in (12,70 m); length, 28 ft 2½ in (8,60 m); height, 9 ft 2¼ in (2,80 m); wing area, 181·9 sq ft (16,90 m²).

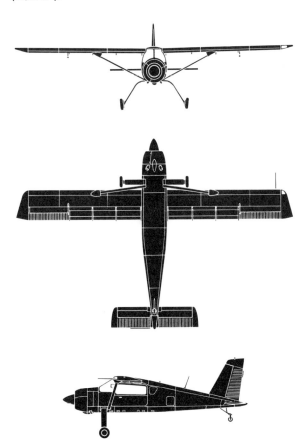

SAAB 39 GRIPEN

Country of Origin: Sweden.
Type: Single-seat multi-role fighter.
Power Plant: One 12,250 lb st (54·5 kN) dry and 18,100 lb st (80·5 kN) General Electric/Volvo Flygmotor RM 12 (F404-GE-400) turbofan.
Performance: No data have been released at the time of closing for press, but maximum speed is expected to range from 914 mph (1 470 km/h) at sea level, or Mach = 1·2, to 1,450 mph (2 555 km/h) above 36,000 ft (10 975 m), or Mach = 2·2.
Weights: Estimated clean loaded, 17,635 lb (8 000 kg).
Armament: One 27-mm Mauser BK 27 cannon and (intercept) four Rb 72 Sky Flash and two Rb 24 Sidewinder AAMs, or (attack) various electro-optically-guided ASMs, conventional or retarded bombs, or RBS 15F anti-shipping missiles.
Status: First of five prototypes flown on 9 December 1988, with the fifth prototype flying on 23 October 1991. Initial contract for 30 series aircraft with first production aircraft (to be retained for test purposes) flying during 1992, and initial deliveries scheduled for 1993. A decision concerning a second production series of 110 aircraft was anticipated mid 1992.
Notes: The Gripen (Griffon) was designed to fulfil fighter, attack and reconnaissance tasks with all necessary hardware and software for these missions being carried permanently. The official designation of JAS 39 signifies its three roles (ie, *Jakt/Attack/Spaning*, or Fighter/Attack/Reconnaissance), and a tandem two-seat training version, the JAS 39B, was under consideration at the beginning of 1992. The Gripen makes extensive use of composites and features a triple-redundant digital fly-by-wire control system. An improved version, the JAS 39C, is being proposed for a third production series.

SAAB 39 GRIPEN

Dimensions: (Approximate) Span, 26 ft 3 in (8,00 m); length, 46 ft 3 in (14,00 m); height, 15 ft 5 in (4,70 m).

SAAB 340B

Country of Origin: Sweden.
Type: Regional commercial and corporate transport.
Power Plant: Two 1,870 hp (1,394 kW) General Electric CT7-9B turboprops.
Performance: Max cruise speed, 325 mph (522 km/h) at 15,000 ft (4 575 m), 322 mph (519 km/h) at 20,000 ft (6 100 m); range cruise, 290 mph (467 km/h) at 25,000 ft (7 620 m); max initial climb, 2,050 ft/min (10,41 m/sec); range with 45 min reserves (35 passengers), 1,123 mls (1 807 km), (30 passengers), 1,509 mls (2 427 km) at range cruise.
Weights: Operational empty, 17,715 lb (8 036 kg); max take-off, 28,500 lb (12 927 kg).
Accommodation: Flight crew of two and optional regional airline seating arrangements for 33, 35 or 37 passengers three abreast.
Status: First (SF 340) prototype flown 25 January 1983 and first production (4th aircraft) 340A flown on 5 March 1984. Production switched from 340A to 340B in August 1989 at No 160, initial delivery of the latter taking place in the following September. Deliveries of the 340A and B totalled some 280 by the beginning of 1992, when firm orders had been placed for 366 aircraft with 274 delivered to 32 operators, and production was running at 50 annually.
Notes: The 340B is a 'hot and high' version of the 340A, which replaced the initial version in production late in 1987 after completion of 160 Saab 340As, which had 1,735 shp (1 294 kW) CT7-5A2 engines. Corporate and VIP variants are available, that used by the Swedish Air Force being designated Tp 100 (illustrated).

Dimensions: Span, 70 ft 4 in (21,44 m); length, 64 ft 8½ in (19,72 m); height, 22 ft 8 in (6,91 m); wing area, 450 sq ft (41,81 m²).

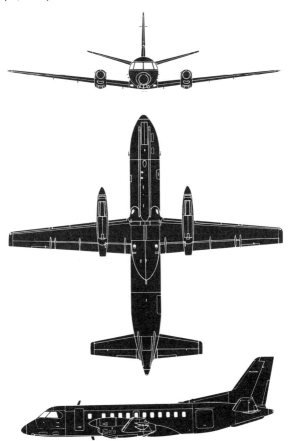

SAAB 2000

Country of Origin: Sweden.

Type: Short-haul regional transport.

Power Plant: Two 3,650 shp (2 722 kW) (including automatic power reserve) Allison GMA 2100A turboprops.

Performance: Max cruise speed, 421 mph (678 km/h) at 25,000 ft (7 620 m); range cruise, 345 mph (556 km/h) at 31,000 ft (9 450 m); max initial climb, 2,320 ft/min (11,8 m/sec); service ceiling, 31,000 ft (9 450 m); range with 50 passengers and typical reserves, 1,550 mls (2 492 km).

Weights: Operational empty, 28,000 lb (12 700 kg); max take-off, 47,000 lb (21 320 kg).

Accommodation: Flight crew of two. Typical layout for 50 passengers three-abreast. Max seating for 58, three abreast.

Status: Final definition and marketing launch in December 1988. First flight, 26 March 1992. Firm orders for 46 and options for 146 by early 1992, placed by more than 16 customers. Launch order for 25 (plus 25 options) placed by Crossair, with deliveries to begin in September 1993.

Notes: The Saab 2000 evolved from extensive studies of possible stretched derivatives of the Saab 340. It has the same fuselage cross section and same basic wing structure, but a lengthened fuselage and increased wing span. Emphasis placed on cruising speed and high initial rate of climb allows Saab to claim that the 2000 will compete in performance with forthcoming regional jets, whilst offering greater economy of operation. Saab contracted with CASA in Spain to complete detailed design and undertake production of the entire wing of the Saab 2000. Valmet in Finland is responsible for the vertical and horizontal tail surfaces and Westland in the UK manufactures the rear fuselage, leaving Saab responsible for the remainder of the fuselage and for assembly, installation of systems and equipment, and flight testing.

SAAB 2000

Dimensions: Span, 81 ft 3 in (24,76 m); length, 88 ft 8 in (27,03 m); height, 25 ft 4 in (7,73 m); wing area, 600 sq ft (55,74 m²).

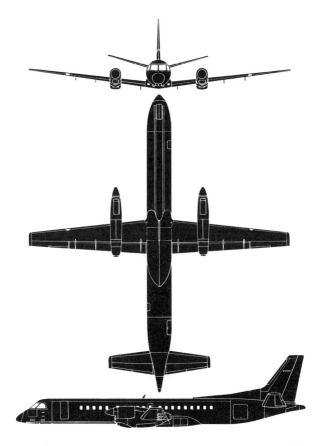

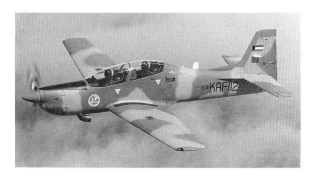

SHORTS S312 TUCANO

Country of Origin: United Kingdom (Brazil).
Type: Tandem two-seat basic trainer.
Power Plant: One 1,100 shp (820 kW) Garrett TPE331-12B turboprop.
Performance: Max speed (at 5,732 lb/2 600 kg), 315 mph (507 km/h) at 10,000–15,000 ft (3 050–4 575 m); normal cruise, 276 mph (448 km/h); econ cruise, 253 mph (407 km/h); max initial climb, 3,510 ft/min (17,38 m/sec); range (with 30 min reserves), 1,035 mls (1 665 km), (with external fuel), 2,061 mls (3 317 km) at 25,000 ft (7 620 m).
Weights: Basic empty (aerobatic), 4,447 lb (2 017 kg); max take-off (aerobatic), 6,393 lb (2 900 kg), (weapons configuration), 7,716 lb (3 500 kg).
Status: Brazilian-built prototype flown on 14 February 1986, with first Shorts-built aircraft following on 30 December that year, deliveries to the RAF (against order for 130) commencing on 16 June 1988. In addition, 12 have been supplied to Kenya (as T Mk 51s) and 16 to Kuwait (as T Mk 52s).
Notes: Derived from the EMB-312 (which see) specially to meet an RAF requirement, the S312 Tucano Mk 1 has a more powerful engine, structural strengthening to extend fatigue life, a ventral air brake and a revised cockpit layout, the Shorts- and Embraer-built Tucanos possessing only 25 per cent commonality. The export T Mk 51s and 52s have enhanced avionics, upgraded air conditioning and provision for up to 2,205 lb (1 000 kg) of external ordnance distributed between four wing stations.

SHORTS S312 TUCANO

Dimensions: Span, 37 ft 0 in (11,28 m); length, 32 ft 4¼ in (9,86 m); height, 11 ft 1⅞ in (3,40 m); wing area, 208·07 sq ft (19,33 m²).

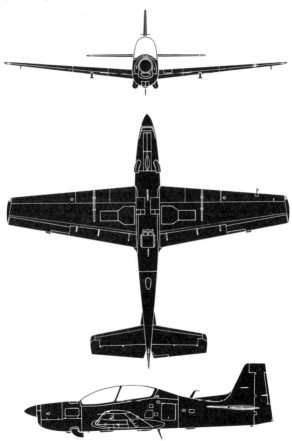

SLINGSBY T67M260 FIREFLY

Country of Origin: United Kingdom.
Type: Military primary training aircraft.
Power Plant: One 260 kp (195 kW) Textron Lycoming AEIO-540-D4A5 six-cylinder horizontally-opposed piston engine.
Performance: Max level speed, 175 mph (281 km/h) at sea level; cruising speed (75 per cent power) at 8,500 ft (2 590 m), 172 mph (277 km/h); max initial climb, 1,600 ft/min (8,1 m/sec); endurance, over 3·5 hrs.
Weights: Approximate empty, 1,560 lb (708 kg); max take-off (utility and aerobatic), 2,450 lb (1 111 kg).
Accommodation: Pilot and student side-by-side.
Status: M260 military version of the basic T67 Firefly completed full flight test programme during 1991. T67A first flew 15 May 1981, certificated 6 October 1981. Military T67M flown on 5 December 1982, certificated 20 September 1983; T67B certificated 18 September 1984; T67M200 flown on 16 May 1985, certificated 13 October 1985; T67M Mk 2 certificated 20 December 1985 and T-67C on 15 December 1987. More than 100 sold, all variants.
Notes: Original T67A was licence-built version of the French Fournier RF-6B, of wooden construction, with 116 hp (86·5 kW) O-235 engine. Slingsby developed an all-composite airframe for later Firefly variants, of which T67B and T67C are for civil flying-school use, the latter with 160 hp (119 kW) AEIO-320 engine. T67M military version also has 160 hp engine, and Mk 2 designation indicates introduction of two-piece canopy. T67M200 has 200 hp (149 kW) AEIO-360 engine and T67M260 (described above) was developed to meet USAF requirement for an Enhanced Flight Screener (EFS) to be used to assess and 'stream' candidates for military flying training.

SLINGSBY T67M260 FIREFLY

Dimensions: Span, 34 ft 9 in (10,6 m); length, 24 ft 10 in (7,55 m); height, 7 ft 9 in (2,36 m); wing area, 136 sq ft (12,62 m²).

SOCATA TBM 700

Country of Origin: France.

Type: Light business and executive transport.

Power Plant: One 700 shp (522 kW) Pratt & Whitney Canada PT6A-64 turboprop.

Performance: Max speed, 345 mph (556 km/h) at 26,000 ft (7 925 m); normal cruise, 325 mph (523 km/h) at 30,000 ft (9 145 m); range cruise, 281 mph (452 km/h) at 30,000 ft (9 145 m); max range (six passengers), 1,180 mls (1 900 km); (max fuel), 1,925 mls (3 100 km).

Weights: Standard empty, 3,946 lb (1 790 kg); max take-off, 6,580 lb (2 985 kg).

Accommodation: Pilot and co-pilot/passenger on flight deck and up to six passengers in main cabin, typical arrangement being for four passengers with club seating.

Status: First of three prototypes flown on 14 July 1988, with second and third following on 3 August and 11 October 1989. First production aircraft flown on 24 August 1990. Total commitments for approximately 100 TBM 700s by early 1992, of which more than 70 on firm order. Production rate four per month in 1991.

Notes: The TBM 700 was developed in France by Socata (the general aviation subsidiary of Aérospatiale) with a one-third participation by Mooney Aircraft in the USA. TBM SA was set up on a 70/30 shared basis by Socata and Mooney to market the aircraft and to manage shared production, but Mooney withdrew from the programme in May 1991.

Dimensions: Span, 39 ft 10¾ in (12,16 m); length, 34 ft 2½ in (10,43 m); height, 13 ft 1 in (3,99 m); wing area, 193·7 sq ft (18,00 m²).

SUKHOI SU-24 (FENCER)

Country of Origin: Commonwealth of Independent States (Russia).

Type: Two-seat (MK) deep penetration interdictor and strike, (MR) reconnaissance and electronic warfare, (MP) electronic jamming and signals intelligence aircraft.

Power Plant: Two 17,200 lb st (76·5 kN) dry and 24,800 lb st (110·5 kN) NPO Saturn (Lyulka) AL-21F-3A turbojets.

Performance: (MK) Max speed (clean), 1,440 mph (2 317 km/h) above 36,090 ft (11 000 m), or Mach = 2·18, 820 mph (1 320 km/h) at 4,920 ft (1 500 m), or Mach = 1·15; tactical radius (HI-LO-HI with two 275 Imp gal/1 250 l drop tanks and 6,615 lb/3 000 kg ordnance), 650 mls (1 050 km); max range, 1 553 mls (2 500 km).

Weights: Empty equipped, 41,885 lb (19 000 kg); normal loaded, 79,365 lb (36 000 kg); max take-off, 87,523 lb (39 700 kg).

Armament: One six-barrel 23-mm rotary cannon and max external stores load of 17,635 lb (8 000 kg).

Status: First prototype Su-24 (T-6-21 or T-62) flown in 1969, and pre-series model deployed with trials unit in 1974, first operational version attaining service status in 1976. Total production exceeded 800 aircraft by the beginning of 1992 at which time it was continuing at Komsomolsk at reduced rate of approximately 30 annually.

Notes: The principal service versions of the Su-24 at the beginning of 1992 were the Su-24MK (*Fencer-D*) introduced in 1983, the Su-24MR (*Fencer-E*) reconnaissance and electronic warfare version which entered service in 1985, and the Su-24MP (*Fencer-F*) electronic jamming and signals intelligence model that appeared in service in 1987. The Su-24 has been exported to Iran, Iraq, Libya and Syria.

Dimensions: Span (16 deg sweep), 57 ft 10 in (17,63 m), (68 deg sweep), 34 ft 0 in (10,36 m); length (including probe), 80 ft 5¾ in (24,53 m); height, 16 ft 3¾ in (4,97 m); wing area, 452 sq ft (42,00 m²).

SUKHOI SU-25T (FROGFOOT)

Country of Origin: Commonwealth of Independent States (Russia).

Type: Single-seat anti-armour aircraft.

Power Plant: Two 9,921 lb st (44·18 kN) MNPK Soyuz (Tumansky) R-195 turbojets.

Performance: Max speed, 606 mph (975 km/h) at sea level, or Mach = 0·8; service ceiling, 22,965 ft (7 000 m); range (with 11,023 lb/5 000 kg ordnance load and two external tanks), 560 mls (900 km) at sea level, 932 mls (1 500 km) at altitude.

Weights: (Estimated) Empty equipped, 22,000 lb (9 980 kg); normal loaded, 33,000 lb (14 970 kg); max take-off, 40,000 lb (18 145 kg).

Armament: One twin-barrel 30-mm cannon and up to 11,023 lb (5 000 kg) of ordnance distributed between eight wing pylons. Two additional wing pylons outboard for two R-60 (*Aphid*) self-defence missiles. Typical loads include two X-58 (*Kilter*) anti-radiation missiles and two packs each containing eight X-25ML Vikhr laser-guided missiles.

Status: First of three flying prototypes of the Su-25T flown in August 1984, these being followed by a pre-series of 10 aircraft which were undergoing evaluation in 1991. Offered for export as the Su-25TK.

Notes: The Su-25T is an upgraded development of the basic Su-25 design, production of the single-seat version of which was phased out in 1991 with more than 330 delivered. Based on the airframe of the two-seat Su-25UB operational conversion and weapons trainer, the Su-25T has new digital navigational and targeting systems, incorporating automated electro-optical, laser designator and laser rangefinding facilities. Versions of the basic Su-25 include the single-seat Su-25K export model and Su-25BM target tug, and two-seat Su-25UT and UTG, the former lacking the weapons capability of the UB and the latter being an experimental deck landing trainer with arrester gear.

Dimensions: Span, 47 ft 1½ in (13,36 m); length, 50 ft 4¾ in (15,36 m); height, 15 ft 9 in (4,80 m); wing area, 362·75 sq ft (33,70 m²).

SUKHOI SU-27 (FLANKER)

Country of Origin: Commonwealth of Independent States (Russia).

Type: Single-seat all-weather counterair fighter and (Su-27UB) combat-capable two-seat conversion trainer.

Power Plant: Two 27,575 lb st (123·85 kN) afterburning Saturn (Lyulka) AL-31F turbofans.

Performance: Max speed, 1,550 mph (2 500 km/h) above 36,100 ft (11 000 m), or Mach = 2·35, 835 mph (1 345 km/h) at sea level, or Mach = 1·1; service ceiling, 59,055 ft (18 000 m); combat radius (subsonic intercept mission with four R-27 and four R-73 AAMs), 930 mls (1 500 km); range (with max fuel), 2,485 mls (4 000 km).

Weights: Normal loaded, 48,500 lb (22 000 kg); max take-off, 66,135 lb (30 000 kg).

Armament: One 30-mm six-barrel rotary cannon and up to 10 AAMs on fuselage tandem pylons, beneath the engine ducts, beneath the outer wings and at each wing tip, a typical mix comprising four R-60 *Aphid* or R-73 *Archer* close-range IR missiles and six R-27 *Alamo* (two short-burn semi-active radar *Alamo-A*, two short-burn IR-homing *Alamo-B* and two long-burn semi-active radar *Alamo-C*) medium- and long-range AAMs.

Status: Prototype (T-10) flown on 20 May 1977, followed by extensively redesigned prototype on 20 April 1981, this (*Flanker-B*) entering production in 1982–83 at Komsomolsk, with initial operational capability achieved 1986.

Notes: The two-seat Su-27UB *Flanker-C* (illustrated above) retains full combat capability, two having been supplied to China, together with 22 single-seaters, with deliveries completed early 1992. A shipboard version, the Su-27K *Flanker-D* with folding outer wing panels, foreplanes, revised undercarriage, arrester hook and flight refuelling capability, has been flown from the Russian carrier *Admiral Kuznetsov*. A side-by-side two-seat attack version, the Su-27IB, has been tested.

SUKHOI SU-27 (FLANKER)

Dimensions: Span, 48 ft 2¾ in (14,70 m); length (excluding probe), 71 ft 11½ in (21,93 m); height, 19 ft 5½ in (5,93 m); wing area (approx), 680 sq ft (63,20 m²).

SWEARINGEN SJ30

Country of Origin: USA.

Type: Light corporate executive transport.

Power Plant: Two 1,900 lb st (8·6 kN) Williams International FJ44 turbofans.

Performance: (Manufacturer's estimates) Max cruise speed, 512 mph (824 km/h); range cruise, 475 mph (765 km/h); max operating altitude, 41,000 ft (12 500 m); max range (IFR), 1,990 mls (3 205 km), (VFR), 2,390 mls (3 845 km).

Weights: Empty equipped, 5,700 lb (2 586 kg); max take-off, 9,850 lb (4 469 kg).

Accommodation: Pilot and co-pilot/passenger on flight deck and standard main cabin arrangement for four passengers in individual seats in facing pairs. Optional arrangements for up to six passengers.

Status: First prototype entered flight test on 13 February 1991. Second (series) prototype for certification to fly in 1992. First production SJ30 to fly late 1992 and certification expected third quarter of 1993.

Notes: An advanced-technology 'low cost' corporate transport intended to compete with turboprop-powered aircraft of similar capacity, the SJ30 developed by Swearingen Engineering and Technology was to have been marketed by Gulfstream Aerospace as the SA-30 Gulfjet. Gulfstream withdrew from the project on 1 September 1989, its place being taken by the Jaffe Group, but Jaffe also withdrew in 1990 and Swearingen arranged to produce the SJ30 in a new facility at Kent County Aero Park in Dover, Delaware. The two prototypes were built at San Antonio, Texas.

Dimensions: Span, 36 ft 4 in (11,07 m); length, 42 ft 4 in (12,9 m); height, 12 ft 11 in (3,94 m); wing area, 164·9 sq ft (15,32 m²).

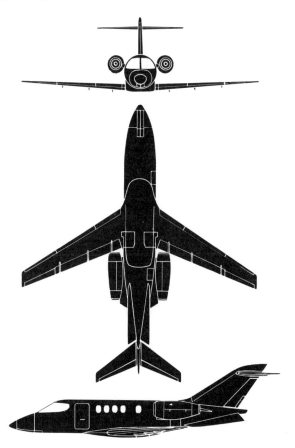

TUPOLEV TU-22M-3 (BACKFİRE-C)

Country of Origin: Commonwealth of Independent States (Russia).

Type: Medium-range strategic bomber and maritime strike/ reconnaissance aircraft.

Power Plant: Two (estimated) 35,000 lb st (155·67 kN) dry and 50,000 lb st (222·27 kN) afterburning KKBM (Kuznetsov) turbofans.

Performance: (Estimated) Max speed (short period dash), 1,320 mph (2 124 km/h) at 39,370 ft (12 000 m), or Mach = 2·0, (sustained), 1,090 mph (1 755 km/h), or Mach = 1·65; combat radius (unrefuelled high-altitude subsonic mission profile), 2,160 mls (4 200 km).

Weights: (Estimated) Max take-off, 285,000 lb (129 275 kg).

Armament: One twin-barrel GSh-23 cannon in remotely-controlled tail barbette. Primary armament of two AS-4 (K-22) *Kitchen* inertially-guided stand-off missiles on wing centre section pylons, or single AS-4 semi-recessed on fuselage centreline, plus AS-9 *Kyle* anti-radar missiles and/or AS-16 *Kickback* short-range attack missiles. Optional loads include up to 26,450 lb (12 000 kg) of conventional bombs internally.

Status: The Tu-22M (alias Tu-26) is believed to have entered flight test in 1971, the first series version, the Tu-22M-2 (*Backfire-B*), achieving operational capability in 1977–78. The more advanced Tu-22M-3 (*Backfire-C*) followed from 1985, production continuing at Kazan at beginning of 1992 when long-established rate of 30 per annum was being halved.

Notes: The Tu-22M-3 introduced wedge-type engine air intakes, and, at the beginning of 1992 some 160–170 of this version of *Backfire* were reportedly included in the inventories of both the air forces and naval air arm of the Commonwealth of Independent States.

TUPOLEV TU-22M-3 (BACKFIRE-C)

Dimensions: (Estimated) Span (20 deg sweep), 112 ft 6 in (34,30 m), (65 deg sweep), 76 ft 9 in (23,40 m); length, 130 ft 0 in (39,62 m); height, 35 ft 6 in (10,80 m); wing area, 1,800 sq ft (167,22 m²).

TUPOLEV TU-160 (BLACKJACK)

Country of Origin: Commonwealth of Independent States (Russia).

Type: Long-range strategic bomber.

Power Plant: Four 30,865 lb st (137·28 kN) dry and 55,115 lb st (245·14 kN) afterburning KKBM (Kuznetsov) NK-321 turbofans.

Performance: Max (over-target dash) speed, 1,254 mph (2 020 km/h) at 36,090 ft (11 000 m), or Mach = 1·9; max continuous speed, 1,056 mph (1 700 km/h), or Mach = 1·6; range cruise, 497 mph (800 km/h) at 45,930 ft (14 000 m); max range (unrefuelled), 7,456 mls (12 000 km).

Weights: Max take-off, 606,260 lb (275 000 kg).

Armament: Two 32·8-ft (10,00 m) weapons bays with rotary dispensers capable of carrying a total of 35,935 lb (16 300 kg) of ordnance. Alternative internal loads include 12 1,865-mile (3 000-km) range AS-15 (RKV-500) *Kent* subsonic low-altitude cruise missiles, or 24 AS-16 (BL-10) *Kickback* supersonic short-range attack missiles.

Status: The Tu-160, evolved through the *Samolyot* (Aircraft) 70 programme, entered flight test on 19 December 1981, with series production commencing at Kazan in 1984, peaking at 30 aircraft per annum in 1990 and thereafter reducing to 15–17 annually by early 1992 when some 55 had been delivered against anticipated total production of 100 aircraft.

Notes: The 14th production Tu-160 was utilised to establish FAI-recognised speed-with-load and altitude-with-load records on 31 October and 3 November 1989.

TUPOLEV TU-160 (BLACKJACK)

Dimensions: Span (20 deg sweep), 182 ft 9 in (55,70 m), (65 deg sweep), 110 ft 9 in (33,75 m); length, 177 ft 6 in (54,10 m); height, 42 ft 11¾ in (13,10 m).

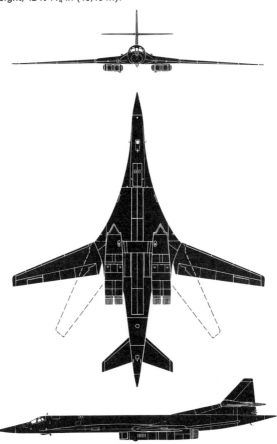

TUPOLEV TU-204-100

Country of Origin: Commonwealth of Independent States (Russia).

Type: Medium-haul commercial transport.

Power Plant: Two 35,275 lb st (156·9 kN) Perm (Soloviev) PS-90A turbofans.

Performance: (At 206,125 lb/93 500 kg) Max cruise speed, 528 mph (850 km/h) at 35,000 ft (10 650 m); econ cruise, 503 mph (810 km/h) at 40,000 ft (12 200 m); range (with max fuel and 196 passengers), 2,392 mls (3 850 km) at 515 mph (828 km/h) at 36,100 ft (11 000 m).

Weights: Operational empty, 124,560 lb (56 500 kg); max take-off, 219,356 lb (99 500 kg).

Accommodation: Flight crew of two (with optional flight engineer) with maximum of 214 passengers four abreast in all-economy class arrangement. Typical basic single-aisle arrangement for 12 first-class four abreast and 35 business-class and 143 economy-class passengers six abreast.

Status: First of five flying prototypes flown on 2 January 1989, the second in August 1990 and three more by the end of 1991. First three production aircraft in final assembly early 1992. Aeroflot requirement for 350 aircraft of this type with service entry expected in second half of 1992.

Notes: The Soviet counterpart to the Boeing 757, the Tu-204 has triple inertial navigation systems and a wing of supercritical section. The -100 is to be followed by -200 with a maximum weight of 239,200 lb (108 500 kg). Tupolev plans to fly Tu-204s with trial installations of the Rolls-Royce RB211-535E4 and the Pratt & Whitney PW2037, with testing expected to begin in June 1992 and 1993 respectively. Also expected to fly in 1992, the Tu-334 has a shorter fuselage of the same cross-section, a similar but smaller wing and two rear-fuselage-mounted Zaporozhye/Lotarev D-436T turbofans.

Dimensions: Span, 137 ft 9½ in (42,00 m); length, 151 ft 7¾ in (46,22 m); height, 45 ft 6½ in (13,88 m); wing area, 1,815 sq ft (168,6 m²).

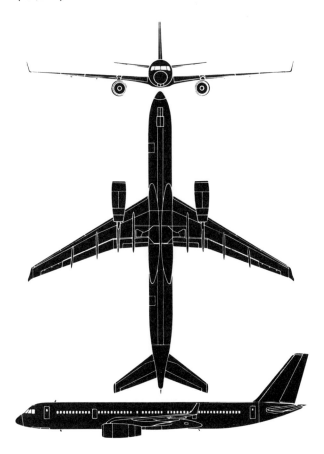

VALMET L-90 TP REDIGO

Country of Origin: Finland.

Type: Two/four-seat multi-purpose primary/basic training and liaison aircraft.

Power Plant: One 500 shp (373 kW) Allison 250-B17F turboprop flat rated at 420 shp (313 kW).

Performance: Max speed, 258 mph (415 km/h) at 5,000 ft (1 525 m); max cruise, 219 mph (352 km/h) at 7,875 ft (2 400 m); cruise (75% power), 194 mph (312 km/h); max initial climb, 1,771 ft/min (9,0 m/sec); time to 16,400 ft (5 000 m), 11 min; range (max internal fuel and 30 min reserves), 870 mls (1 400 km) at 19,685 ft (6 000 m).

Weights: Empty equipped, 2,094 lb (950 kg); max take-off (aerobatic), 2,976 lb (1 350 kg), (utility with external stores), 4,189 lb (1 900 kg).

Armament: (Weapons training and light strike) Max external load of 1,764 lb (800 kg) distributed between six underwing stations, the two inboard stations each being stressed for 551 lb (250 kg) and remaining four being stressed for 331 lb (150 kg).

Status: First of two prototypes flown on 1 July 1986, and second (with Turboméca TP 319 engine) on 3 December 1987. Deliveries against a Finnish Air Force contract for 10 aircraft began in 1992.

Notes: The Vinka may be fitted with a second pair of seats in the rear of the cabin permitting configuration for liaison and observation tasks, other potential roles including photographic, target towing and search and rescue missions.

VALMET L-90 TP REDIGO

Dimensions: Span, 34 ft 9¼ in (10,60 m); length, 27 ft 11¾ in (8,53 m); height, 10 ft 6 in (3,20 m); wing area, 158·77 sq ft (14,75 m²).

YAKOVLEV YAK-42 (CLOBBER)

Country of Origin: Commonwealth of Independent States (Russia).

Type: Short-medium-range jetliner.

Power Plant: Three 14,330 lb st (63·74 kN) Zaporozhye/Lotarev D-36 turbofans.

Performance: Max cruising speed, 503 mph (810 km/h) at 25,000 ft (7 600 m); best economy cruise, 460 mph (740 km/h); range with max payload, 808 mls (1 300 km) at 460 mph (740 km/h) at 29,500 ft (9 000 m); range with max passenger load, 1,180 mls (1 900 km).

Weights: Empty equipped, 76,236 lb (34 580 kg); max take-off, 124,560 lb (56 500 kg).

Accommodation: Flight crew of two. Standard arrangement (Yak-42D) for 120 passengers six abreast with central aisle, at 29·5-in (75-cm) pitch.

Status: First of three prototypes flown 7 March 1975. First production aircraft flown 1980, and Aeroflot services began at the end of that year. In production, with about 100 built for Aeroflot including 20 Yak-42Ds. First exports early 1992, to China and Cuba. First flight by Yak-42E-LL test-bed 15 March 1991.

Notes: The Yak-42 was developed primarily to replace the Tu-134 on Aeroflot's domestic routes. The first prototype had only 11 deg of wing sweepback but subsequent prototypes and the production aircraft have 23 deg of sweepback and production Yak-42s differ from prototypes in having four-wheeled main landing gear bogies. The Yak-42D, introduced in 1990, featured increased wing fuel capacity, systems improvements and gross weight increased from 119,000 lb (54 000 kg) to 124,560 lb (56 500 kg). The Yak-42F carries pods under each wing for electro-optical tasks and the Yak-42E-LL is an engine test-bed with a Progress/Lotarev D-236 propfan in the starboard side nacelle.

214

YAKOVLEV YAK-42 (CLOBBER)

Dimensions: Span, 114 ft 5¼ in (34,88 m); length, 119 ft 4¼ in (36,38 m); height, 32 ft 3 in (9,83 m); wing area, 1,615 sq ft (150 m²).

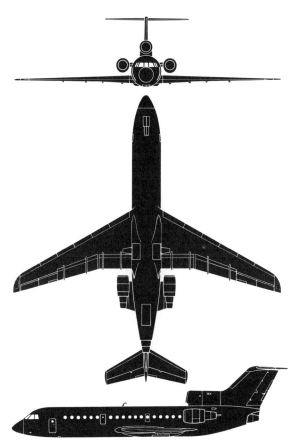

YAKOVLEV YAK-141 (FREESTYLE)

Country of Origin: Commonwealth of Independent States (Russia).

Type: Single-seat shipboard V/STOL multi-role fighter.

Power Plant: One 19,840 lb st (88·25 kN) dry and 34,170 lb st (152 kN) afterburning Soyuz (Khachaturov/Koptchyenko) R-79 vectored-thrust turbofan and two 9,390 lb st (41·75 kN) RKBM RD-41 lift turbojets.

Performance: Max speed, 1,118 mph (1 800 km/h) above 36,090 ft (11 000 m), or Mach = 1·69; service ceiling, 49,200+ ft (15 000+ m); range (VTO), 870 mls (1 400 km), (STO with external fuel), 1,305 mls (2 100 km).

Weights: Max loaded (STO), 42,989 lb (19 500 kg).

Armament: One 30-mm GSh-301 cannon and mix of AA-8 *Aphid* (R-60T) and AA-11 *Archer* (R-73) IR-homing and AA-10 *Alamo* (R-27) radar-guided AAMs. Max external weapons load of 5,732 lb (2 600 kg).

Status: The first of two flying prototypes flown in March 1989, with flight test programme continuing through 1991, but further development uncertain at beginning of 1992.

Notes: The world's second supersonic V/STOL combat aircraft (the first having been the Dassault Mirage IIIV), the Yak-141 has been optimised for air defence with secondary ground attack capability. Making extensive use of aluminium/lithium in its construction, with 26 per cent of the airframe by weight being of composite construction, the Yak-141 has a digital full-authority triplex fly-by-wire control system with an hydraulic servo back-up. The afterburning thrust of the R-79 engine is reduced to 27,336 lb st (121·6 kN) in the hover mode in which it is balanced by the two lift engines mounted in tandem immediately aft of the pilot's cockpit.

YAKOVLEV YAK-141 (FREESTYLE)

Dimensions: Span, 33 ft 1⅔ in (10,10 m); length (including probe), 60 ft 0 in (18,30 m); height, 16 ft 5 in (5,00 m).

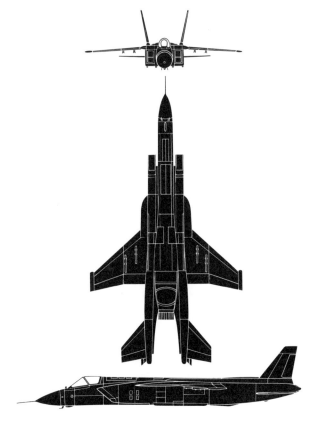

AGUSTA A 109A MK II PLUS

Country of Origin: Italy.
Type: Light multi-role helicopter.
Power Plant: Two 450 shp (335 kW) Allison 250-C20R-1 turboshafts.
Performance: (At 5,732 lb/2 600 kg) Max cruise speed at 6,000 ft (1 830 m), 175 mph (281 km/h); max inclined climb, 1,655 ft/min (8,4 m/sec); hovering ceiling (in ground effect), 12,465 ft (3 800 m), (out of ground effect), 8,530 ft (2 600 m); max range, 506 mls (815 km); max endurance, 4·5 hrs.
Weights: Empty, 3,157 lb (1 432 kg); max take-off, 5,732 lb (2 596 kg).
Dimensions: Rotor diam, 36 ft 1 in (11,00 m); fuselage length, 35 ft 1½ in (10,71 m).
Notes: The Mk II Plus is the latest version of the basic A 109A, which first flew on 4 August 1971 and has been in continuous production since 1974. It is available in commercial, military, naval and law enforcement versions. Primarily for the US market, the A 109C has composite rotor blades and increased transmission rating, whilst the A 109MAX is optimised for the medevac mission. The A 109K2 is a development specifically for 'hot and high' operations, with 737 shp (550 kW) Turboméca Arriel IKI turboshafts. The A 109KM military version with Arriel engines may be fitted with a HeliTow launch system for up to eight TOW wire-guided missiles, a pintle-mounted 7,62-mm gun and a door gunner post with a 12,7-mm gun. Delivery of 28 TOW-armed A 109HA and 18 scouting A 109HO helicopters to the Belgian Army was under way in 1992, from SABCA.

AGUSTA A 129 MANGUSTA

Country of Origin: Italy.
Type: Two-seat light anti-armour, attack and scout helicopter.
Power Plant: Two 825 shp (615 kW) Rolls-Royce Gem 2 Mk 1004D turboshafts.
Performance: (At 8,488 lb/3 850 kg) Max speed, 171 mph (275 km/h) at sea level; max continuous cruise, 155 mph (250 km/h); max inclined climb, 2,025 ft/min (10·29 m/sec); hovering ceiling (in ground effect), 10,300 ft (3 140 m), (out of ground effect), 6,200 ft (1 890 m); max ceiling, 15,500 ft (4 725 m); range, 328 mls (528 km); endurance, 3·075 hrs.
Weights: Empty, 5,575 lb (2 529 kg); normal loaded (anti-armour configuration), 8,488 lb (3 850 kg); max take-off, 9,039 lb (4 100 kg).
Dimensions: Rotor diam, 39 ft 0½ in (11,90 m); fuselage length, 40 ft 3¼ in (12,27 m).
Notes: The Mangusta (Mongoose) was developed to meet an Italian Army requirement, the first of five flying prototypes entering flight test on 11 September 1983. After lengthy development, the first five production helicopters were accepted by the Army in October 1990, when it was scheduled for a further 10 to follow in 1991, within an overall total requirement for 60. Development of a scout version with a mast-mounted sight is planned, to meet an additional Italian Army requirement for 30, but budgetary constraints may restrict production of this version. One of the prototype A 129s was fitted with LHTEC T800 turboshafts in 1988. A utility passenger/cargo version has been proposed as the A 139.

BELL MODEL 206L-3 LONGRANGER III

Country of Origin: USA.

Type: Seven-seat light utility helicopter.

Power Plant: One 650 shp (485 kW) Allison 250-C30P turbo-shaft.

Performance (at 4,150 lb/1 882 kg): Max cruise at 5,000 ft (1 525 m), 126 mph (203 km/h); max inclined climb, 1,340 ft/min (6,8 m/sec); hovering ceiling (in ground effect), 16,500 ft (5 030 m), (out of ground effect), 5,400 ft (1 645 m); service ceiling, 20,000 ft (6 100 m); range (no reserves, at 5,000 ft/1 525 m), 414 mls (666 km).

Weights: Standard empty, 1,635 lb (742 kg); max take-off, 3,200 lb (1 451 kg).

Dimensions: Rotor diam, 33 ft 4 in (10,16 m); fuselage length, 31 ft 2 in (9,50 m).

Notes: The LongRanger, which was announced by Bell in 1973, is one of the many derivatives of the original Bell Model 206. The 206B-3 and 206L-3, respectively JetRanger III and LongRanger III, are the final derivatives, the latter having a lengthened rear fuselage that adds some 4 ft (1,2 m) to allow two more seats in the cabin. Bell Textron transferred production of these two helicopters to its Canadian facility at Mirabel, Quebec, in 1986 and production in 1991 was at a combined rate of some 15 per month. Production of the commercial JetRanger totals more than 4,250 up to 1992, and of the LongRanger more than 1,150. A LongRanger conversion with two 450 shp (335 kW) Allison 250-C20Rs is marketed by Tridair Helicopters as the Gemini ST.

BELL MODEL 230

Country of Origin: USA (Canada).
Type: Six/ten-seat light utility and transport helicopter.
Power Plant: Two 700 shp (522 kW) Allison 250-C30G2 turboshafts.
Performance: Max cruise speed, 161 mph (259 km/h), (utility), 157 mph (252 km/h); range, 379 mls (609 km), (utility), 484 mls (780 km); endurance, 2·4 hrs, (utility), 3·0 hrs.
Weights: Empty (utility), 4,903 lb (2 224 kg); max take-off, 8,250 lb (3 742 kg).
Dimensions: Rotor diam, 42 ft 0 in (12,80 m); fuselage length, 42 ft 6¾ in (12,97 m).
Notes: The Model 230 is a derivative of the Model 222 which it is intended to replace, production of the latter having ended with 184 built. Two of these were transferred to Bell's Canadian company in 1990 for conversion to prototypes of the Bell Model 230 and the first of these flew at Mirabel, Quebec, on 12 August 1991. The major difference between the two models is the use of Allison engines in the 230 in place of Textron Lycoming LTS 101 turboshafts, but the latter engines probably will be offered as an option after the initial batch of 50 Model 230s has been built. The Model 230 will be available in both fixed-skid and retractable-wheel versions, and it is likely that the two-bladed rotor will be replaced by a four-bladed rotor. It is also expected that, subsequent to the 15th production helicopter, Bell's liquid inertia vibration elimination system (LIVE) will be adopted. Bell expects to certificate the 230 in March 1992 with first deliveries in August. Eight will be built in 1992 and 24 in 1993.

BELL MODEL 406 (OH-58D)

Country of Origin: USA.

Type: Two-seat light multi-purpose military helicopter.

Power Plant: One 650 shp (485 kW) Allison 250-C30R turboshaft.

Performance: (OH-58D at 4,500 lb/2 041 kg) Max speed 147 mph (237 km/h) at 4,000 ft (1 220 m); max cruise, 138 mph (222 km/h) at 2,000 ft (610 m); max inclined climb, 1,540 ft/min (7,8 m/sec); hovering ceiling (in ground effect), 12,000+ ft (3 660 + m), (out of ground effect), 11,200 ft (3 415 m); range (no reserves), 345 mls (556 km).

Weights: Empty, 2,825 lb (1 281 kg); max take-off (OH-58D), 4,500 lb (2 041 kg), (Kiowa Warrior), 5,500 lb (2 495 kg).

Dimensions: Rotor diam, 35 ft 0 in (10,67 m); fuselage length, 33 ft 10 in (10,31 m).

Notes: The Model 406 is a major upgrade of the US Army's OH-58A Kiowa, the first of five prototypes having flown on 6 October 1983. The US Army programme covered 227 OH-58As upgraded to armed OH-58D plus 16 new-build OH-58Ds to Kiowa Warrior standard, with mast-mounted sight and provision for four Hellfire air-to-surface or Stinger air-to-air missiles, two seven-round 2·75-in rocket pods or 7,62-mm or 12,7-mm gun pods. All OH-58Ds are eventually to be brought up to full Kiowa Warrior standard and 81 of these will be further modified to Multi-Purpose Light Helicopter (MPLH) configuration. The USMC is also to acquire 30 OH-58D conversions. The Model 406 CS (Combat Scout) is a simplified variant of OH-58D, of which 15 were supplied to Saudi Arabia as MH-58Ds in 1990.

BELL MODEL 412SP

Country of Origin: USA (Canada).

Type: Fifteen-seat utility transport helicopter.

Power Plant: One 1,400 shp (1 044 kW) Pratt & Whitney Canada PT6T-3B-1 Turbo Twin Pac twin turboshaft.

Performance: (At 11,900 lb/5 397 kg) Max Cruise, 143 mph (230 km/h); max inclined climb, 1,350 ft/min (6,86 m/sec); service ceiling, 16,500 ft (5 030 m); hovering ceiling (in ground effect), 9,200 ft (2 895 m), (out of ground effect at 10,500 lb/ 4 762 kg), 9,200 ft (2,805 m); max range (standard fuel, no reserves), 408 mls (656 km) at sea level.

Weights: Empty (utility), 6,495 lb (2 946 kg); max take-off, 11,900 lb (5 397 kg).

Dimensions: Rotor diam, 46 ft 0 in (14,02 m); fuselage length, 42 ft 4¾ in (12,92 m).

Notes: Derived from the Model 212, the Model 412 entered flight test in August 1979 and became Bell's first helicopter with a four-bladed rotor to enter production, with customer deliveries commencing on 18 January 1981. The Model 412SP (Special Performance) featured an uprated transmission and an increased maximum take-off weight. Licence manufacture of the Model 412SP is undertaken in Indonesia by IPTN and in Italy by Agusta, all production by the parent company having been transferred from the USA to Canada early in 1989. Agusta has developed a multi-purpose military version named Griffon, and the parent company has developed both a military version of the Model 412SP and a version with improved transmission, the Model 412HP, has been ordered (100) for the Canadian Forces.

BELL AH-1W SUPERCOBRA

Country of Origin: USA.
Type: Two-seat light anti-armour and attack helicopter.
Power Plant: Two 1,625 shp (1 213 kW) General Electric T700-401 turboshafts.
Performance: (At 14,750 lb/6 690 kg) Max speed, 196 mph (315 km/h) at sea level; max cruise, 173 mph (278 km/h); hovering ceiling (in ground effect), 14,750 ft (4 495 m), (out of ground effect), 3,000 ft (9,15 m); range (standard fuel), 365 mls (587 km) at sea level with standard fuel.
Weights: Empty, 10,200 lb (4 627 kg); max take-off, 14,750 lb (6 690 kg).
Dimensions: Rotor diam, 48 ft 0 in (14,63 m); fuselage length, 45 ft 6 in (13,87 m).
Notes: First flown on 16 November 1983, the AH-1W SuperCobra is an enhanced-capability derivative of the US Marine Corps' AH-1T SeaCobra, all surviving examples of which have been upgraded to -1W standard. Forty-four AH-1Ws were ordered for the USMC early in 1984, after testing of a prototype (converted AH-1T) had begun on 16 November 1983. Further orders followed and the 100th AH-1W was delivered on 8 August 1991, with production continuing. The USMC Reserves received 42 AH-1W SuperCobra conversions from AH-1Ts in 1990–91, and five AH-1Ws were supplied to the Turkish Army in 1990, with four to follow in 1991. One AH-1W has been fitted with a four-bladed bearingless rotor as the AH-1-(4B)W Viper, first flown on 24 January 1989, and a similar rotor is being developed for possible retrofit to the USMC AH-1W fleet.

BOEING HELICOPTERS CH-47D CHINOOK

Country of Origin: USA.

Type: Medium transport helicopter.

Power Plant: Two 4,378 shp (3 264 kW) Textron Lycoming T55-L-712 SSB or 5,028 shp (3 749 kW) T55-L-714 turboshafts.

Performance: (L-714 engines, at 54,000 lb/24 494 kg) Max speed, 185 mph (298 km/h); average cruise speed, 153 mph (246 km/h); hovering ceiling (out of ground effect), 7,930 ft (2 415 m); max range (normal fuel), 150 mls (241 km); max fuel range, 363 mls (585 km).

Weights: Typical empty, 23,574 lb (10 693 kg); max take-off, 54,000 lb (24 494 kg).

Dimensions: Rotor diam (each), 60 ft 0 in (18,29 m); fuselage length, 51 ft 0 in (15,54 m).

Notes: The CH-47D designation identifies the US Army upgrade of 472 Chinooks built as CH-47A, B or C models in the 'sixties. First CH-47D prototype flew on 11 May 1979 and first 'production' conversion on 26 February 1982. Up to 51 MH-47E Chinooks (see 1991/92 edition) are to be procured by US Army for Special Operations Forces as conversions of CH-47Ds, the first of which flew on 1 June 1990. Model 414-100 International Chinook is similar to CH-47D with some additional improvements, higher weights (as quoted above) and more powerful engine option. As CH-47J, the Model 414-100 is built in Japan by Kawasaki, and at least 15 other nations have procured Chinooks of earlier types, including some licence-built by Agusta in Italy. Boeing has on-going programmes in 1992 to upgrade Chinooks to CH-47D standard for Spain and the UK.

EH INDUSTRIES EH 101 (MERLIN)

Countries of Origin: United Kingdom and Italy.

Type: Military and commercial transport, utility and shipboard anti-submarine warfare helicopter.

Power Plant: Three (Merlin) 2,312 shp (1 566 kW) Rolls-Royce Turboméca RTM 322 or (Italian Navy) 1,714 shp (1 278 kW) General Electric T700-GE-T6A or (NSA) 2,000 shp (1 491 kW) CT7-6A1 turboshafts.

Performance: (CT7-6 engines) Typical cruise speed, 169 mph (272 km/h); best endurance speed, 104 mph (167 km/h); range (standard fuel and 30 passengers), 633 mls (1 019 km).

Weights: Empty operational (naval), 20,500 lb (9 275 kg), (military utility), 19,000 lb (8 618 kg), (commercial), 19,220 lb (8 718 kg); max take-off (naval), 29,830 lb (13 530 kg), (military and commercial), 31,500 lb (14 288 kg).

Dimensions: Rotor diam, 61 ft 0 in (18,59 m); fuselage length, 64 ft 0 in (19,51 m).

Notes: Developed by EH Industries, in which Westland Helicopters of the UK and Agusta of Italy collaborate, the EH 101 is to be of single-source manufacture with final assembly lines in both the UK and Italy. Nine prototypes have flown, the first on 9 October 1987 and the last on 16 January 1991. These represent the basic airframe, the British and Italian naval ASW/ASV versions, the military and commercial transport with rear loading ramp and civil Heliliner 30-seat transport (illustrated). Orders/commitments are likely for 50 Merlin HAS Mk 1s for the Royal Navy, 42 for the Italian Navy, 35 for the Canadian NSA programme and 25 utility transports for the RAF.

ENSTROM MODEL 480 (TH-28)

Country of Origin: USA.

Type: Three/four-seat light utility helicopter.

Power Plant: One 420 shp (313 kW) Allison 250-C20W turboshaft.

Performance: Max cruise speed, 121 mph (195 km/h); economical cruise, 104 mph (167 km/h); max inclined climb, 1,220 ft/min (6,2 m/sec); service ceiling, 15,000 ft (4 570 m); hovering ceiling (in ground effect), 10,400 ft (3 170 m), (out of ground effect), 4,200 ft (1 280 m); max range, 380 mls (611 km).

Weights: Empty, 1,560 lb (707 kg); max take off, 2,700 lb (1 225 kg).

Dimensions: Rotor diameter, 32 ft 0 in (9,75 m); fuselage length, 29 ft 4 in (8,95 m).

Notes: Model 480 is the appellation of the basic four-seat civil version of Enstrom's latest derivative of a helicopter that dates back to 1959, when the original Enstrom company was founded. TH-28 refers to a three-seat variant proposed in the US Army competition for a new training helicopter for its initial entry rotary wing/training system (IERW/TS) in 1992. Evolution of the Model 480/TH-28 began with the installation of an Allison turboshaft in a piston-engined Enstrom 280FX Shark, which flew for the first time in December 1989. This was followed on 7 October 1989 by a prototype TH-28 with the definitive cockpit configuration which features three-across seating for instructor, student pilot and observing student. Enstrom held orders for at least 40 Model 480s by early 1992, when production by Enstrom of all its helicopter types combined was at the rate of 36 a year.

EUROCOPTER TIGER

Countries of Origin: France and Germany.
Type: Tandem two-seat anti-armour and ground support helicopter.
Power Plant: Two 1,285 shp (958 kW) MTU/Rolls-Royce/ Turboméca MTR 390 turboshafts.
Performance: (Estimated at 11,905 lb/5 400 kg) Max cruise, 174 mph (280 km/h); normal cruise, 155 mph (250 km/h); max inclined climb, 1,970+ ft/min (10+ m/sec); hovering ceiling (out of ground effect), 6,560+ ft (2 000+ m); endurance (including 20 min reserves), 2·85 hrs.
Weights: Basic empty, 7,275 lb (3 300 kg); mission take-off, 11,685–12,786 lb (5 300–5 800 kg); max overload, 13,227 lb (6 000 kg).
Dimensions: Rotor diam, 42 ft $7\frac{3}{4}$ in (13,00 m); fuselage length, 45 ft $11\frac{1}{4}$ in (14,00 m).
Notes: The Tiger is being developed by Eurocopter International, which merges the helicopter interests of Aérospatiale in France and Deutsche Aerospace in Germany. As a joint Franco-German programme, the Tiger is projected in three versions: the HAC Tigre and HAP Gerfaut for the French Army, for escort and for anti-tank tasks respectively; and the PAH-2 Tiger anti-tank helicopter for the German Army. Estimated requirements are 75 HAPs and 140 HACs for France and 138 PAH-2s for Germany. The first of five prototypes (PT1) flew at Marignane on 17 April 1991 in 'baseline' configuration. PT2, an HAP Gerfaut, was to fly in mid-1992, with first deliveries of the Gerfaut in 1994, the Tiger in 1999 and the Tigre in 1998.

EUROCOPTER (AEROSPATIALE) AS 332/532 SUPER PUMA MK II/COUGAR MK II

Country of Origin: France.

Type: Multi-role (AS 332) and military (AS 532) helicopter.

Power Plant: Two 1,843 shp (1 374 kW) Turboméca Makila 1A2 turboshafts with emergency rating of 1,959 shp (1 461 kW).

Performance: (AS 532) Max speed, 196 mph (315 km/h); cruise, 172 mph (276 km/h) at sea level; max inclined climb, 1,279 ft/min (6,5 m/sec); hovering ceiling (in ground effect), 8,200 ft (2 500 m), (out of ground effect), 5,200 ft (1 585 m); range (standard tankage), 402 mls (647 km).

Weights: Empty, 10,251 lb (4 650 kg); max take-off, 20,944 lb (9 500 kg), (with slung load), 22,046 lb (10 000 kg).

Dimensions: Rotor diam, 53 ft 1¾ in (16,2 m); fuselage length, (tail rotor included), 55 ft 1 in (16,79 m).

Notes: The AS 332 Super Puma Mk II and the AS 532 Cougar Mk II are respectively civil and military versions of the same basic helicopter and, compared with the Mk I versions, have longer main rotor blades and lengthened rear fuselage. The Super Puma Mk II development vehicle first flew on 6 February 1987. Current version is the AS 332 L2, deliveries of which to Bristow Helicopters began in April 1992. The Cougar Mk II is the tactical support AS 532 A2 with 20-mm cannon or rocket launchers, and the AS 532 U2 transport and medevac helicopter. Atlas in South Africa has added features of the AS 532, including the engines and airframe improvements, to SAAF AS 330 Pumas to produce the Gemsbok (illustrated).

EUROCOPTER (AEROSPATIALE) AS 350/550
ECUREUIL/FENNEC

Country of Origin: France.

Type: Five/six-seat light general-purpose helicopter.

Power Plant: One 724 shp (540 kW) Turboméca Arriel 1D1 turboshaft.

Performance: (AS 550 at 4,850 lb/2 200 kg) Max speed, 178 mph (287 km/h); cruise, 155 mph (249 km/h) at sea level; max inclined climb, 1,988 ft/min (10,1 m/sec); hovering ceiling (in ground effect), 13,300 ft (4 050 m), (out of ground effect), 11,200 ft (3 400 m); range (standard tankage), 426 mls (686 km).

Weights: Empty, 2,601 lb (1 180 kg); max take-off (anti-tank configuration), 5,181 lb (2 350 kg), (with external load), 5,512 lb (2 500 kg).

Dimensions: Rotor diam, 35 ft 0¾ in (10,69 m); fuselage length (tail rotor included), 35 ft 10½ in (10,93 m).

Notes: The AS 350 Ecureuil and AS 550 Fennec are respectively civil and military versions of the same basic helicopter, more than 1,520 having been delivered by the beginning of 1992. A version powered by the Textron Lycoming LTS 101-600A-3 turboshaft is marketed in North America as the AStar and, with the Arriel 1D1 engine, as the SuperStar. The military Fennec (originally AS 350 L2) is available as the AS 550 U2 utility transport, the AS 550 A2 for fire support and aerial combat with airframe reinforcement for axial armament, and the AS 550 C2 anti-armour model with the Saab/Emerson Electric HeliTow anti-tank missile system. The AS 550 M2 and AS 550 S2 are respectively unarmed and armed naval versions.

EUROCOPTER (AEROSPATIALE) AS 355/555
ECUREUIL 2/FENNEC

Country of Origin: France.
Type: Five/six-seat light general-purpose helicopter.
Power Plant: Two 460 shp (343 kW) Allison 250-C20R or 456 shp (340 kW) Turboméca Arrius-IM turboshafts.
Performance: (AS 355N) Max speed, 173 mph (278 km/h); cruise, 140 mph (225 km/h) at sea level; max inclined climb, 1,340 ft/min (6,9 m/sec); hovering ceiling (in ground effect), 8,530 ft (2 600 m), (out of ground effect), 5,085 ft (1 550 m); range (no reserves), 448 mls (722 km) at sea level.
Weights: Empty, 3,046 lb (1 382 kg); max take-off, 5,600 lb (2 540 kg), (with external load), 5,732 lb (2 600 kg).
Dimensions: Rotor diam, 35 ft 0¾ in (10,69 m); fuselage length (tail rotor included), 35 ft 10⅓ in (10,93 m).
Notes: The AS 355 Ecureuil 2 and AS 555 Fennec are respectively the civil and military versions of the helicopter which entered flight test on 28 September 1979 as a twin-engined derivative of the AS 350 Ecureuil. By the beginning of 1992, some 460 had been delivered, of about 500 ordered. The newest version, for delivery from 1992, introduces Arrius engines in place of the Allison 250s in the AS 335F. Military AS 555s are available in UN (utility), AN (armed), MN (naval utility) and SN (naval armed) configuration. For the US market, the Ecureuil 2 is known as the TwinStar, and in Brazil, where it is locally-assembled by Helibras, it is the HB 355 F2 Esquilo – both that name and Ecureuil translating as Squirrel, a name sometimes used for this helicopter in the UK.

EUROCOPTER (AEROSPATIALE) AS 365 N2 DAUPHIN 2

Country of Origin: France.
Type: Commercial 10/14-seat general-purpose helicopter.
Power Plant: Two 733 shp (547 kW) Turboméca Arriel 1C2 turboshafts.
Performance: Max speed, 184 mph (296 km/h); max cruise, 176 mph (283 km/h); econ cruise, 161 mph (260 km/h); max inclined climb, 1,379 ft/min (7,0 m/sec); hovering ceiling (in ground effect), 8,365 ft (2 550 m), (out of ground effect), 5,905 ft (1 800 m); range (standard fuel), 557 mls (897 km).
Weights: Empty equipped, 4,970 lb (2 254 kg); max take-off, 9,370 lb (4 250 kg).
Dimensions: Rotor diam, 39 ft 2 in (11,94 m); fuselage length (tail rotor included), 38 ft 1⅞ in (11,63 m).
Notes: The AS 365 was flown as a prototype on 31 March 1979, and the standard production version in 1992 is the AS 365 N2, deliveries having commenced in mid-1990. The AS 365 is licence-built in China as the Harbin Z-9, and a modified version for the US Coast Guard is designated AS 366G-1 (HH-65A Dolphin). Deliveries of all versions of the Dauphin 2 (including Chinese production) totalled some 540 by the beginning of 1992. The HH-65A, of which 99 were delivered to the USCG, is powered by 680 shp (507 kW) Textron Lycoming LTS 101-750A-1 turboshafts. In 1993, Aérospatiale expects to begin deliveries of the AS 365 N3 version, which will have the Arriel 2 engine, a five-bladed Spheriflex rotor and EFIS. The new rotor was flown for the first time on 20 March 1989.

EUROCOPTER (AEROSPATIALE) AS 565 PANTHER

Country of Origin: France.
Type: Multi-role light military helicopter.
Power Plant: Two 748 shp (558 kW) Turboméca Arriel 1M1 turboshafts.
Performance: Max speed, 184 mph (296 km/h), cruise, 172 mph (277 km/h) at sea level; max inclined climb, 1,378 ft/min (7,0 m/sec); hovering ceiling (in ground effect), 8,530 ft (2 600 m), (out of ground effect), 6,070 ft (1 850 m); range (with standard fuel), 544 mls (875 km) at sea level.
Weights: Empty, 4,835 lb (2 193 kg); max take-off, 9,369 lb (4 250 kg).
Dimensions: Rotor diam, 39 ft 2 in (11,94 m); fuselage length (including tail rotor), 39 ft 8¾ in (12,11 m).
Notes: A military development of the Dauphin 2 emphasising survivability in a combat environment, the AS 565 flew as a prototype on 29 February 1984. Composite materials are used exclusively for the dynamic components. The crew seats, control servos and engine controls are armoured. Versions on offer include the utility AS 565 UA, the anti-tank AS 565 CA, the aerial combat and ground attack AS 565 AA (used by Brazil and Angola), the maritime patrol and SAR AS 565 MA and the Exocet-armed ASW AS 565 SA (ordered by Chile). The naval versions were previously known as AS 365 F Dauphin 2s, in which guise examples were sold to Saudi Arabia, Eire and the French Aéronavale. The Panther 800 is a variant with LHTEC T800 engines proposed in the US by LTV with IBM.

EUROCOPTER (MBB) BO 108

Country of Origin: Germany.
Type: Four/five-seat light helicopter.
Power Plant: Two 480 shp (360 kW) Turboméca TM 319 Arrius 1B or 460 shp (342 kW) Pratt & Whitney Canada PW206B turboshafts.
Performance: (Allison 250) Max cruise speed (approx), 168 mph (270 km/h) at 4,920 ft (1 500 m); econ cruise, 149 mph (240 km/h); max inclined climb, 1,810 ft/min (9,23 m/sec); hovering ceiling (in ground effect), 12,630–16,400 ft (3 850–5 000 m), (out of ground effect), 10,990 ft (3 350 m); max range, 497 mls (800 km).
Weights: Empty, 2,700 lb (1 225 kg); max take-off, 5,511 lb (2 500 kg).
Dimensions: Rotor diam, 32 ft 9¾ in (10,00 m), (later) 33 ft 5½ in (10,20 m); fuselage length, 31 ft 9 in (9,68 m).
Notes: The BO 108 is the intended successor to the BO 105, production of which is continuing with more than 1,350 delivered. It was initiated as a technology demonstrator embodying new and advanced features, such as a completely hingeless main rotor, shallow transmission with special vibration absorbers, composite structures, etc. The first prototype was flown on 15 October 1988 with Allison 250 turboshafts, but the Turboméca Arrius has been adopted for the initial production version and the second prototype flew with these engines on 5 June 1991. Two certification examples follow, one each with Arrius and PW206B engines. Initial certification is set for 1994, with full IFR certification and first deliveries in 1995.

EUROCOPTER (MBB/KAWASAKI) BK 117

Countries of Origin: Germany and Japan.

Type: Multi-purpose eight/twelve-seat helicopter.

Power Plant: Two 592 shp (442 kW) Textron Lycoming LTS 101-750B-1 or 660 shp (492 kW) Turboméca Arriel 1-E turboshafts.

Performance: (BK 117B-1 at 7,055 lb/3 200 kg) Max speed, 172 mph (278 km/h) at sea level; max cruise, 154 mph (248 km/h); max inclined climb, 1,910 ft/min (9,7 m/sec); hovering ceiling (in ground effect), 9,600 ft (2 925 m), (out of ground effect), 7,500 ft (2 285 m); range (max standard fuel), 354 mls (570 km).

Weights: Basic empty, 3,807 lb (1 727 kg); max take-off, 7,055 lb (3 200 kg).

Dimensions: Rotor diam, 36 ft 1 in (11,00 m); fuselage length, 32 ft 6¼ in (9,91 m).

Notes: The BK 117 was developed jointly by MBB of Germany, now the Eurocopter Deutschland subsidiary of Deutsche Aerospace, and Kawasaki of Japan. Customer deliveries of the initial BK 117A-1 began early in 1981, the progressively improved A-3 and A-4 finally giving place to the current standard B-1 (and B-1C for UK market). The BK 117C-1 introduces Arriel engines, for deliveries to begin in mid-1992. BK 117M is the military version and NBK-117 is built by IPTN in Indonesia. Jaffe Helicopter in USA is converting B-1s to have 550 shp (410 kW) Lycoming LTS101-650B-1 turboshafts. Some 300 BK 117s of all types had been built in Germany by the beginning of 1992 and some 80 in Japan by Kawasaki.

HAL ALH

Country of Origin: India.
Type: Multi-role civil and military light helicopter.
Power Plant: Two 1,000 shp (746 kW) Turboméca TM 333-2B turboshafts.
Performance: (Estimated) Max speed, 174 mph (280 km/h) at sea level; cruise speed, 152 mph (245 km/h); max inclined climb, 1,770 ft/min (9,0 m/sec); hovering ceiling (out of ground effect), 9,850+ ft (3 000+ m); service ceiling, 19,685 ft (6 000 m); range with max fuel (20-min reserve), 497 mls (800 km).
Weights: Empty, 5,511 lb (2 500 kg); max take-off (Army/Air Force), 8,818 lb (4 000 kg), (Navy), 11,023 lb (5 000 kg).
Dimensions: (Approximate) Rotor diam, 43 ft 3¾ in (13,20 m); fuselage length, 42 ft 3¾ in (12,89 m).
Notes: The ALH (Advanced Light Helicopter) was developed by Hindustan Aeronautics Limited (HAL) with the assistance of the Helicopter and Military Aircraft Group (MBB) of Deutsche Aerospace (now Eurocopter Deutschland), and the first was expected to enter flight test mid 1992, with series production commencing 1994. Versions are proposed for the three armed services and the Coast Guard in the capacity of a replacement for the Chetak/Cheetah. The ALH for the Army is intended for air assault, re-supply of heliborne forces, aerial minelaying and anti-tank missions; the Navy version will fulfil CASEVAC, communications, SAR and ASW roles, and the Air Force variant is to perform air crew rescue, off-shore operations, logistical support, light transport and CASEVAC missions.

KAMAN SH-2G SUPER SEASPRITE

Country of Origin: USA.
Type: Shipboard anti-submarine helicopter.
Power Plant: Two 1,723 shp (1 285 kW) General Electric T700-GE-401 turboshafts.
Performance: Max speed at sea level, 159 mph (256 km/h); normal cruise speed, 138 mph (222 km/h); max inclined climb, 2,500 ft/min (12,7 m/sec); hovering ceiling (in ground effect), 20,800 ft (6 340 m); hovering ceiling (out of ground effect), 18,000 ft (5 486 m); service ceiling, 23,900 ft (7 285 m); max range with two external tanks, 500 mls (885 km).
Weights: Empty, 7,600 lb (3 447 kg); max take-off weight, 13,500 lb (6 124 kg).
Dimensions: Rotor diam, 44 ft 4 in (13,51 m); fuselage length, 40 ft 0 in (12,19 m).
Notes: The SH-2G is the latest development of the Kaman helicopter that began life in 1957 under US Navy contract and was first produced in single piston-engined form as the HU2K-1. Many of the 190 built were modified to twin-turbine configuration and 54 more similar SH-2Fs were built between 1983 and 1989. Further upgrading has resulted in the SH-2G, which introduces the T700 engines, composite rotor blades, MIL-STD 1553B digital databus and updated avionics. A converted SH-2F flew as the YSH-2G prototype in April 1985 and, with full avionics, on 28 December 1989. Delivered to the US Navy in 1991, it was followed by six new-build SH-2Gs, the first of which flew in March 1990. The Navy also plans to convert up to 90 SH-2Hs to the newer standard, to equip four squadrons.

KAMOV KA-29TB (HELIX-B)

Country of Origin: Commonwealth of Independent States (Russia).

Type: Assault transport helicopter.

Power Plant: Two 2,225 shp (1,660 kW) NPO Klimov (Isotov) TV3-117VK turboshafts.

Performance: Max speed, 165 mph (265 km/h) at sea level; max cruise, 143 mph (230 km/h); max inclined climb, 2,380 ft/min (12,09 m/sec); normal range, 310 mls (500 km).

Weights: Empty, 12,170 lb (5 520 kg); max take-off, 27,775 lb (12 600 kg).

Dimensions: Rotor diam (each), 53 ft 9½ in (16,40 m); fuselage length (excluding nose probe), 37 ft 8¾ in (11,50 m).

Notes: First displayed publicly in August 1989, and allegedly in series production early 1992, the Ka-29TB is a derivative of the Ka-27 (*Helix-A*) ASW and (*Helix-D*) SAR helicopter and is primarily a transport for seaborne assault troops. Possessing a wider flight deck than that of the Ka-27, and stub wings embodying ordnance pylons, the Ka-29TB is heavily armoured, has a four-barrel rotary 7,62-mm gun behind a downward articulated door in the starboard side of the nose and sensor pods beneath the nose. The wing pylons may carry AT-6 *Spiral* radio-guided tube-launched missiles, or packs of 57-mm or 80-mm rockets. The Ka-29TB can accommodate 14-18 combat-equipped troops on sidewall seats. The Ka-27 (see 1989/90 edition) serves aboard the carriers *Kuznyetsov* and *Varyag* in both *Helix-A* and -*D* forms, and aboard the *Gorshkov* and *Novorossiysk* carrier/cruisers.

KAMOV KA-32 (HELIX-C)

Country of Origin: Commonwealth of Independent States (Russia).

Type: Commercial utility helicopter.

Power Plant: Two 2,225 shp (1,660 kW) NPO Klimov (Isotov) TV3-117VK turboshafts.

Performance: (At 24,250 lb/11 000 kg) Max speed, 155 mph (250 km/h) at sea level; max cruise, 143 mph (230 km/h); hovering ceiling (out of ground effect), 11,480 ft (3 500 m); service ceiling, 19,685 ft (6 000 m); range (with max fuel), 497 mls (800 km); endurance, 4·5 hrs.

Weights: Normal loaded, 24,250 lb (11 000 kg); max flight weight with slung load, 27,775 lb (12 600 kg).

Dimensions: Rotor diam (each), 52 ft 2 in (15,90 m); fuselage length, 37 ft 1 in (11,30 m).

Notes: The Ka-32 is a commercial derivative of the Ka-27 ASW and SAR helicopter, and appeared in prototype form in 1981. Two versions have been produced in series, the Ka-32S (illustrated above) for deployment aboard icebreakers and the Ka-32T basic transport and flying crane. The latter possesses less sophisticated avionics, and its tasks include the transportation of internal and external freight, and of up to 16 passengers on sidewall and rear bulkhead folding seats. The Ka-32S is equipped for operation in adverse weather conditions and over terrain devoid of landmarks. Its tasks include ice patrol, the guidance of ships through icefields, support of offshore drilling rigs, maritime search and rescue, and the loading and unloading of ships. Production was continuing at the beginning of 1992.

KAMOV KA-50 (HOKUM)

Country of Origin: Commonwealth of Independent States (Russia).

Type: Single-seat attack helicopter.

Power Plant: Two 2,225 shp (1,660 kW) Leningrad Klimov (Isotov) TV3-117VK turboshafts.

Performance: Max speed (in shallow dive), 217 mph (350 km/h), (level flight), approx 175 mph (280 km/h) at sea level; hovering ceiling (out of ground effect), 13,125 ft (4 000 m).

Weights: Approx max loaded, 16,500 lb (7 500 kg).

Dimensions: Rotor diam (each), 47 ft 6$\frac{7}{8}$ in (14,50 m); overall length (rotors turning), 52 ft 5$\frac{7}{8}$ in (16,00 m).

Notes: Unique among current helicopters in being a single-seater intended for the attack mission, the Kamov Ka-50, assigned the NATO reporting name *Hokum*, underwent competitive evaluation against the Mil Mi-28 *Havoc* (see 1991/92 edition). The Kamov helicopter, which first entered flight test on 27 July 1982, was chosen as winner of the contest and entered production in 1990. Heavily armoured, it is provided with an ejection seat for the pilot, seat actuation automatically jettisoning the rotor blades. Fixed armament comprises a single 30-mm cannon and main armament is provided by up to 16 AT-9 *Whirlwind* six-mile-range tube-launched anti-armour missiles. These are carried in clusters of eight on stub wings. An alternative warload is provided by packs containing a total of 80 unguided 80-mm rockets, 20 rockets of 130-mm calibre or 16 *Vikhr* laser-guided, beam-riding missiles. A tandem-seat trainer version of the Ka-50 exists.

McDONNELL DOUGLAS AH-64A APACHE

Country of Origin: USA.

Type: Tandem two-seat attack helicopter.

Power Plant: Two 1,696 shp (1,265 kW) General Electric T700-GE-701 turboshafts.

Performance: (At 14,445 lb/6 552kg) Max speed, 184 mph (296 km/h); typical mission cruise (at 15,780 lb/7 158 kg), 169 mph (272 km/h); max inclined climb, 2,500 ft/min (12,7 m/sec); hovering ceiling (in ground effect), 15,000 ft (4 570 m), (out of ground effect), 11,500 ft (3 505 m); max range (internal fuel), 300 mls (482 km).

Weights: Empty, 10,760 lb (4 881 kg); max take-off, 21,000 lb (9 525 kg).

Dimensions: Rotor diam, 48 ft 0 in (14,63 m); fuselage length, 48 ft 1$\frac{7}{8}$ in (14,70 m).

Notes: First of two YAH-64 prototypes of the Apache was flown on 30 September 1975, and deliveries to the US Army of the AH-64A commenced in 1984, with a total of 807 to be completed by December 1993. An upgrade programme will provide 254 conversions to the improved AH-64B standard in 1994–96, and then 308 AH-64Cs with improved crew stations, Hellfire missile capability, plus provision for more powerful -701C engines and Longbow fire-control radar, starting in 1995. Finally, 227 Apaches will become AH-64Ds, from 1996, with all the above features installed. Export orders have been placed by Egypt (24), Greece (12), Israel (18), Korea (37), Kuwait (30), Saudi Arabia (12 plus 36 planned) and United Arab Emirates (20).

McDONNELL DOUGLAS MD 520N

Country of Origin: USA.

Type: Five/seven-seat utility helicopter.

Power Plant: One (derated) 375 shp (280 kW) Allison 250-C20R-2 turboshaft.

Performance: Max cruise speed, 144 mph (230 km/h) at sea level; max inclined climb, 1,546 ft/min (7,9 m/sec); hovering ceiling (in ground effect), 9,300 ft (2 835 m), (out of ground effect), 5,600 ft (1 707 m); service ceiling, 20,000 ft (6 100 m); max range (standard fuel), 242 mls (387 km) at 5,000 ft (1 525 m).

Weights: Empty, 1,586 lb (719 kg); max take-off (normal), 3,350 lb (1 519 kg), (with external load), 3,850 lb (1 746 kg).

Dimensions: Rotor diam, 27 ft 4 in (8,30 m); fuselage length, 25 ft 6 in (7,8 m).

Notes: The MD 520N (described and illustrated above) and the more powerful MD 530N are the first production NOTAR (NO TAil Rotor) helicopters, the latter having an Allison 250-C30 engine derated to 425 shp (317 kW). Evolved respectively from the orthodox tail rotor MD 530 and MD 500, the MD 530N prototype flew on 29 December 1989 and the 520N on 1 May 1990. Production began in 1990 and the first series MD 520N flew on 2 July 1991. The first delivery was made in October 1991, when more than 156 were on firm order. Up to 36 US Army AH-6/MH-6 examples of the MD 500 are scheduled to be converted to NOTAR configuration. Certification of the MD 530N has been postponed, as the performance of the MD 520N meets the requirements of most customers.

McDONNELL DOUGLAS MD900 EXPLORER

Country of Origin: USA.

Type: Eight/ten-seat transport helicopter.

Power Plant: Two 593 shp (442 kW) Pratt & Whitney Canada PW206A or MD 901 605 shp (451 kW) Turboméca Arrius-2C turboshafts.

Performance: Max cruise speed, 170 mph (272 km/h) at sea level; max inclined climb, 3,100 ft/min (15,8 m/sec); hovering ceiling (in ground effect), 15,000 ft (4 572 m), (out of ground effect), 13,000 ft (3 962 m); service ceiling, 20,000 ft (6 100 m); max range, 395 mls (636 km).

Weights: Standard empty, 2,820 lb (1 279 kg); max take-off (normal), 5 600 lb (2 540 kg), (with external load), 6 260 lb (2 839 kg).

Dimensions: Rotor diam, 33 ft 10 in (10,32 m); fuselage length, 31 ft 8 in (9,7 m).

Notes: McDonnell Douglas Helicopters formally launched the MD 900 as the MDX in January 1989 in the small-to-medium size commercial helicopter field. Using technology developed for the MD 520N, the MD 900 is the first helicopter designed from the outset to have NOTAR (NO TAil Rotor), for which enhanced directional control, improved safety and reduced external noise levels are among the claimed advantages. First flight of the MD 900 is set for fourth quarter 1992, to be followed by VFR certification in November 1993 and IFR certification a year later, under FAR Part 27. With production expected to reach a rate as high as nine a month by 1996, the MD 900 attracted close to 300 'certificates of interest' prior to first flight.

MIL MI-26 (HALO)

Country of Origin: Commonwealth of Independent States (Russia).

Type: Military and commercial heavy-lift helicopter.

Power Plant: Two 11,240 shp (8,380 kW) ZMKB Progress (Lotarev) D-136 turboshafts.

Performance: Max speed, 183 mph (295 km/h); normal cruise, 158 mph (255 km/h); hovering ceiling (in ground effect), 14,765 ft (4 500 m), (out of ground effect), 5,905 ft (1 800 m); range (at 109,127 lb/49 500 kg), 310 mls (500 km), (at 123,457 lb/ 56 000 kg), 497 mls (800 km).

Weights: Empty, 62,169 lb (28 200 kg); normal loaded, 109,227 lb (49 500 kg); max take-off, 123,457 lb (56 000 kg).

Dimensions: Rotor diam, 104 ft 11⅞ in (32,00 m); fuselage length, 110 ft 7¾ in (33,73 m).

Notes: First flown on 14 December 1977, the Mi-26 remains the heaviest and most powerful helicopter yet to achieve production status. Limited production was continuing at the beginning of 1992, when an uprated version with all-composite rotor blades and a 48,500-lb (22 000-kg) maximum payload was under development. The current model has a crew of five and a four-seat passenger compartment aft of the flight deck, possible loads including some 85 combat-equipped troops, 40 casualty stretchers plus medical attendants, two airborne infantry combat vehicles or a 44,090-lb (20 000-kg) freight container. The Mi-26 attained operational capability in 1985, some 60–70 reportedly being in service with the armed forces of the Commonwealth of Independent States and others with the Indian Air Force.

PZL SWIDNIK W-3 SOKOL

Country of Origin: Poland.

Type: Medium transport and multi-role helicopter.

Power Plant: Two 880 shp (662 kW) PZL-10W (Omsk/ Glushenkov TVD-10B) turboshafts with emergency rating of 1,134 shp (845·5 kW) for 2·5 min.

Performance: Max speed, 158 mph (255 km/h); max cruise, 146 mph (235 km/h); econ cruise, 137 mph (220 km/h); max inclined climb, 1,673 ft/min (8·5 m/sec); hovering ceiling (in ground effect), 9,845 ft (3 000 m), (out of ground effect), 6,890 ft (2 100 m); range (standard fuel and 5% reserves), 422 mls (680 km), (auxiliary fuel and 5% reserve), 721 mls (1 160 km).

Weights: Basic operational empty, 8,002 lb (3 630 kg); normal take-off, 13,448 lb (6 100 kg); max take-off, 14,110 lb (6 400 kg).

Dimensions: Rotor diam, 51 ft 6 in (15,70 m); fuselage length, 46 ft 7½ in (14,21 m).

Notes: The Sokol (Falcon) was the subject of protracted development, the first of five prototypes having flown on 16 November 1979 but full certification being achieved only on 10 April 1990, after considerable modification of the original design. Series production was initiated in 1990 for the Polish Air Force and to meet a Soviet order for 35. By early 1992, some 50 W-3s had been built, including six for the Myanmar (Burma) Air Force, which has ordered 20–30. Polish requirements include 12 of the Anakonda SAR variant for the Naval Aviation (photo) and an unknown quantity of the Salamanda armed assault version for Army Aviation, carrying twin GSh-23 cannon plus AT-6 Spiral missiles and/or 80-mm rocket pods.

ROBINSON R22 BETA

Country of Origin: USA.

Type: Two-seat light utility helicopter.

Power Plant: One 131 hp (97,5 kW) derated Textron Lycoming O-320-B2C four-cylinder horizontally-opposed piston engine.

Performance: Max speed, 112 mph (180 km/h); cruise speed (75% power), 110 mph (177 km/h) at 8,000 ft (2 440 m); max inclined climb, 1,200 ft/min (6,1 m/sec); service ceiling, 14,000 ft (4 265 m); hovering ceiling (in ground effect), 6,970 ft (2 125 m); range (max payload and auxiliary fuel), 368 mls (592 km).

Weights: Empty, 835 lb (379 kg); max take-off, 1,370 lb (621 kg).

Dimensions: Rotor diam, 25 ft 2 in (7,67 m); fuselage length, 20 ft 8 in (6,30 m).

Notes: The R22 was flown in prototype form for the first time on 28 August 1975, production deliveries commencing in October 1979, and it has since been in continuous production in progressively improved versions. The 2,000th R22 was delivered in November 1991, when production was at eight a week. The first military sale was achieved in the same month, when the Turkish Army ordered ten. The R22 Beta was preceded by 500 of the R22 Alpha version. There is also a float-equipped R22 Mariner and a law-enforcement version known as the R22 Police. Apollo Helicopter Services has developed a belly tank and a 24-ft (7,3-m) spray boom for agricultural use of the R22. A further option provides a load-carrying hook kit complete with electric and mechanical emergency releases.

SCHWEIZER 330

Country of Origin: USA.

Type: Three/four-seat light utility helicopter.

Power Plant: One 200 shp (149 kW) flat-rated Allison 250-C20.

Performance: (At 2,050 lb/930 kg) Max cruise speed, 115 mph (185 km/h); normal cruise, 105 mph (169 km/h); hovering ceiling (in ground effect), 18,000 ft (5 485 m), (out of ground effect), 14,000 ft (4 265 m); max range (no reserves), 255 mls (410 km) at 4,000 ft (1 220 m).

Weights: Empty, 1,050 lb (476 kg); max take-off, 2,050 lb (930 kg); (with external load), 2,150 lb (975 kg).

Dimensions: Rotor diam, 26 ft 10 in (8,18 m); overall length, 30 ft 10 in (9,40 m).

Notes: The Model 330, the prototype of which made its first public flight on 14 June 1988, uses most of the systems, controls, rotors and dynamic components of the piston-engined Model 300C, all rights in which were acquired by Schweizer from the McDonnell Douglas Helicopter company in November 1986. Apart from using a turboshaft, the Model 330 differs from its predecessor in having a totally reconfigured forward fuselage, a tail boom fairing and new vertical tail surfaces. For the instructional role, three seats are provided and flight controls may be fitted at all three seat positions. It is anticipated that the Model 330 will be marketed for a variety of duties, and it is being promoted for the US Army New Training Helicopter requirement. Deliveries (to Crescent Airways, for tuna-spotting off Florida) were to begin during 1992.

SIKORSKY (S-80) MH-53E SEA DRAGON

Country of Origin: USA.

Type: Mine countermeasures helicopter.

Power Plant: Three 4,380 shp (3 266 kW) General Electric T64-GE-416 turboshafts.

Performance: (At 56,000 lb/25 400 kg) Max speed, 196 mph (315 km/h) at sea level; max continuous cruise, 173 mph (278 km/h); max inclined climb (with 25,000-lb/11 340-kg payload), 2,500 ft/min (12,7 m/sec); hovering ceiling (in ground effect), 11,550 ft (3 520 m), (out of ground effect), 9,500 ft (2 895 m); service ceiling, 18,500 ft (5 640 m).

Weights: Empty, 36,336 lb (16 482 kg); max take-off, 69,750 lb (31 640 kg), (with external load), 73,500 lb (33 340 kg).

Dimensions: Rotor diam, 79 ft 0 in (24,08 m); fuselage length, 73 ft 4 in (22,35 m).

Notes: The MH-53E is an airborne mine countermeasures helicopter based on the CH-53E Super Stallion amphibious assault and transport helicopter used by the US Marine Corps and Navy. First flown on 1 March 1974, the CH-53E was itself derived from the twin-engined S-65 series, more than 300 of which were built. USN and USMC requirements for the CH-53E/MH-53E total some 234. Retrofit of the 4,750 shp (3 545 kW) T64-GE-419 engines is planned to begin in 1994. The Japanese Maritime Self-Defence Force is procuring 12 examples of the Sea Dragon designated S-80M, the first of these having been handed over on 30 November 1989. The first MH-53E pre-production model for the US Navy flew for the first time on 1 September 1983, and deliveries began on 26 June 1986.

SIKORSKY (S-70A) UH-60L BLACK HAWK

Country of Origin: USA.
Type: Tactical utility transport helicopter.
Power Plant: Two 1,940 shp (1 448 kW) General Electric T700-GE-701C turboshafts.
Performance: (At 17,432 lb/7 907 kg) Max cruise, 183 mph (295 km/h) at 2,000 ft (610 m); max inclined climb, over 3,000 ft/ min (15,2 m/sec); hovering ceiling (out of ground effect), 11,125 ft (3 390 m); service ceiling, 19,150 ft (5 837 m).
Weights: Empty, 11,516 lb (5 225 kg); max take-off, 22,000 lb (9 979 kg); max weight with external load, 23,000 lb (10 433 kg).
Dimensions: Rotor diam, 53 ft 8 in (16,23 m); fuselage length, 50 ft 0¾ in (15,26 m).
Notes: The S-70A designation covers tactical utility versions of the Black Hawk assault transport developed for the US Army and first flown on 17 October 1974. A total of 985 UH-60As was built before production switched to the UH-60L (illustrated), with uprated engines and much improved mission capability. Variants supplied to the US Army include the EH-60C ('Quick Fix') electronic countermeasures helicopter, and the MH-60A and MH-60K special operations helicopters. The VH-60N is a US Marine Corps-operated VIP transport version and the MH-60G Pave Hawk is a USAF rescue variant. Export models include the Desert Hawk for Saudi Arabia, S-70A-5 for Philippines, S-70A-9 for RAAF, S-70A-17 for Turkey, S-70A for Jordan, VH-60 for Egypt, UH-60L for Bahrain and UH-60P for South Korea, where assembly takes place. The S-70B, developed from the S-70A, is described on page 250.

SIKORSKY (S-70B) HH-60J JAYHAWK

Country of Origin: USA.
Type: Medium range recovery (SAR) helicopter.
Power Plant: Two 1,900 shp (1 417 kW) General Electric T700-GE-401C turboshafts.
Performance: Max speed, 174 mph (280 km/h); max cruise, 168 mph (271 km/h) at sea level; mission endurance, 45 min at 300 mls (483 km) from base.
Weights: Empty, 13,417 lb (6 086 kg); max take-off weight, 21,246 lb (9 637 kg).
Dimensions: Rotor diam, 53 ft 8 in (16,36 m); fuselage length, 52 ft 1 in (15,87 m).
Notes: Jayhawk is the US Coast Guard's name for the HH-60J version of the S-70B, which designation identifies the naval development of the original S-70A Black Hawk for the US Army. First HH-60J flew on 8 August 1989 and the first acceptance and delivery to the USMC (of the second production aircraft) was made on 30 March 1990. Initial operational capability was achieved on 3 July 1991 and 35 are on order, for delivery to be completed by 1993. Jayhawk carries a four-man crew and can recover six survivors. Other members of the S-70B series include the original SH-60B Seahawk anti-submarine and anti-surface vessel helicopters; SH-60F Ocean Hawk ('CV-Helo') inner-zone ASW helicopter, and HH-60H strike-rescue/special warfare support helicopter, all for the US Navy. Export versions of the SH-60B include SH-60J and UH-60J for Japan (with manufacture by Mitsubishi), S-70B for Australia, Greece and Spain, and S-70C for Taiwan.

SIKORSKY S-76C

Country of Origin: USA.

Type: Light general purpose and transport helicopter.

Power Plant: Two 723 shp (540 kW) Turboméca Arriel 1S1 or (S-76B) 981 shp (732 kW) Pratt & Whitney Canada PT6B-36A turboshafts.

Performance: Max speed, 178 mph (287 km/h) at sea level; max cruise, 167 mph (269 km/h); max inclined climb, 1,460 ft/min (7,4 m/sec); service ceiling, 11,800 ft (3 505 m); range with standard fuel (30-min reserve), 421 mls (678 km) at 3,000 ft (915 m).

Weights: Standard empty, 6,282 lb (2 849 kg); max take-off, 11,700 lb (5 306 kg).

Dimensions: Rotor diam, 44 ft 0 in (13,41 m); fuselage length, 43 ft 4½ in (13,22 m).

Notes: The S-76 12-passenger commercial helicopter was flown on 13 March 1977, customer deliveries of the initial version commencing early in 1979. The S-76 Mk II, introduced in March 1982, embodied numerous refinements and its Allison 250-C30 turboshafts had a five per cent higher take-off rating at 650 shp (522 kW). The S-76B, which first flew on 22 June 1984, differed primarily in having PT6B-36 turboshafts and higher gross weight, and the S-76A+ offered Arriel turboshafts as a retrofit and in unsold new S-76As, first flying with these engines in 1987. The S-76C (illustrated) has the basic airframe and drive-train of the S-76B mated with Arriel 1S1 turboshafts. The military H-76 Eagle derivative is in production in South Korea, following delivery of first seven by Sikorsky in 1990/91.

WESTLAND BATTLEFIELD LYNX

Country of Origin: United Kingdom.

Type: Multi-role military helicopter.

Power Plant: Two 1,120 shp (835 kW) Rolls-Royce Gem 42-1 turboshafts.

Performance: Max continuous cruise speed, 159 mph (256 km/h); max endurance speed, 81 mph (130 km/h); max inclined climb, 1,970 ft/min (10 m/sec); range (tactical transport), 426 mls (685 km); anti-tank mission endurance, 2 hrs at 29 mls (46 km).

Weights: Operational empty (anti-tank mission), 8,707 lb (3 949 kg); max take-off, 11,300 lb (5 125 kg).

Dimensions: Rotor diam, 42 ft 0 in (12,80 m); length (rotors folded), 43 ft 5¼ in (13,24 m).

Notes: An upgraded version of the basic Westland helicopter, Battlefield Lynx is the first land-based variant to feature a wheeled undercarriage in place of skids. A naval equivalent, the HAS Mk 8, is known as Super Lynx (see 1991/92 edition). The first wheeled prototype, a converted British Army AH Mk 7, flew on 29 November 1989. Starting in 1991, the Army received 16 new aircraft and eight Mk 7 conversions as AH Mk 9s. A Battlefield Lynx 800 with LHTEC T800 turboshafts flew during October 1991. The Super Lynx has been supplied to South Korea as the Lynx Mk 99 (first flown on 16 November 1989) and this has Seaspray Mk 3 radar and can carry four Sea Skua or two Penguin anti-ship missiles. Five Super Lynx Mk 95 are also being supplied to Portugal, two being conversions of ex-RN Lynx HAS Mk 3s and the others new-built.

INDEX OF AIRCRAFT TYPES